The Art *of* Mindful Singing

Notes on Finding Your Voice

Jeremy Dion

Leaping Hare Press

This paperback edition published in the UK and North America in 2018 by

Leaping Hare Press

An imprint of The Quarto Group
The Old Brewery, 6 Blundell Street
London N7 9BH, United Kingdom
T (0)20 7700 6700 **F** (0)20 7700 8066
www.QuartoKnows.com

First published in hardback in 2016

Text copyright © 2016 Jeremy Dion
Design and layout © 2017 Quarto Publishing plc

British Library Cataloguing-in-Publication Data
A catalogue record for this book is available from
the British Library

ISBN: 978-1-78240-647-1

This book was conceived, designed and produced by

Leaping Hare Press

58 West Street, Brighton BN1 2RA, United Kingdom
Publisher SUSAN KELLY
Creative Director MICHAEL WHITEHEAD
Art Director WAYNE BLADES
Editorial Director TOM KITCH
Commissioning Editor MONICA PERDONI
Project Editor FLEUR JONES
Designer GINNY ZEAL
Illustrator MELVYN EVANS

Printed in Slovenia by GPS Group

1 3 5 7 9 10 8 6 4 2

County Council

Libraries, books and more.........

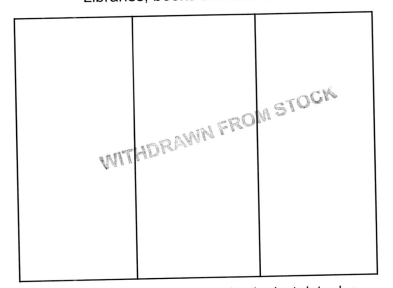

WITHDRAWN FROM STOCK

Please return/renew this item by the last date due.
Library items may also be renewed by phone on
030 33 33 1234 (24 hours) or via our website

www.cumbria.gov.uk/libraries

Cumbria Libraries

Interactive Catalogue

Ask for a CLIC password

CONTENTS

INTRODUCTION

Singing is universally accessible,
which makes it seem like it's really no big deal.
Everyone can sing a little tune, there's nothing to it.
Except that singing is a big deal. Singing can be
transformative. When done with a mindful presence,
singing reconnects us with ourselves, our bodies, our
minds, our emotions, with others and with the Divine.
That's a lot of connecting. Songs become a meditation
in sound, waking us up through a combination of
focus, vibration and breath. Singing brings us
home to ourselves, and provides a pathway
to a more joyful, present life.

SING!

◆

The beauty of something often lies in its simplicity. Like singing. If you can talk, you can sing. It's that simple. Other times, the magic of something lies in its hidden complexity and ever-changing mystery. Like singing. Or love. Or living in the present moment.

HUMAN BEINGS HAVE BEEN BLESSED with many sacred treasures, chief among them breath, awareness and a voice. Of the many ways we use our voices, singing is arguably the most sublime and easily the most frightening form of self-expression. We all have issues with our own voices, whether we are listening to our speaking voices on a recording or judging our singing voices. Singing makes us feel especially vulnerable, and being vulnerable takes courage. So as we embark on this journey into mindful singing, let us summon the courage to become open, to feel present, and to sing.

Everyone is generally capable of singing, but many of us don't. At least not very often, and certainly not in front of other people. The reasons for this self-conscious posture are numerous and multi-layered, some of which we will explore within these pages. But for now, do yourself a favour, set aside your inner critic, and let yourself sing.

The ideas and exercises throughout this book are designed to be both simple and challenging, offering something for fledgling singers as well as seasoned veterans. In addition to singing, the concept of mindfulness – experiencing life in the present moment – is woven throughout. A mindful life is a rich life, and singing is a dynamic and enjoyable way to become more mindful.

Silence the Inner Critic

Many among us have grown shy about our voices. If that doesn't describe you, consider yourself fortunate. Some of us decided a long time ago, or were told, that we couldn't sing, or at least that we couldn't sing very well. So we stopped. And at first blush, that may not seem like a major decision, just another in a long line of things we try out for a while before moving on. But as we will explore in this book, singing is more important than we realize, and the benefits of making it a part of our lives are immense in scope. That decision to stop singing – one few of us even remember making consciously – needs to be revisited. Our happiness may depend on it.

When we learn to silence our inner critic and bring a mindful approach to our bodies and our voices, the more we sing and the better we feel. It's that simple. But don't take my

---

In the beginning was the voice.

Voice is sounding breath, the audible sign of life.

FROM 'LANGUAGE: ITS NATURE, DEVELOPMENT, AND ORIGIN'
OTTO JESPERSEN

---

word for it — try it out. Start singing. Engage with the exercises in this book, commit yourself to singing more in your daily life, and the benefits may surprise you. The list is long indeed, but the truncated version is that singing has the power to connect us with our bodies, open our hearts, move our emotions, express things that wouldn't be expressed otherwise, connect us with the Divine and bring us into the present moment. Singing heals us from the inside. All that and more, just from singing.

The Soundtrack of Our Lives

For me, singing has always been, and continues to be, one of the greatest sources of joy in my life. I sing every single day, even if that means only humming a little tune while I'm doing the dishes. When I'm driving in my car, I'm usually listening to familiar music and singing along. And at home, I make a conscious effort to have music playing more often than the television.

We all deserve our own soundtrack, and it's up to us to create it. Let's start by simply inviting more music into our lives. The digital music revolution has made unimaginably vast catalogues of music available instantaneously at our fingertips through technology like smartphones and savvy apps. It's easier now than ever before to discover new music related to artists you already love, customizing your own free, digital radio stations. We now have any type of music available to us at any point in time with a few taps on the screen, leaving us with no more excuses. It's time to create your own daily soundtrack. It will change your life.

FULL SPECTRUM

Music has the power to transport us, altering our consciousness, opening our hearts and transcending time. Songs can become prayers, carrying our deepest-held hopes and dreams as well as our broken hearts. Our songs tell our stories, and our stories are sacred.

THE HUMAN VOICE IS CAPABLE of producing a staggering variety of tones, pitches and sounds, some of which even mimic those of animals, telephones or other sounds of daily life. A well-trained singing voice is a true marvel, covering a vast vocal range and producing an array of textures and tones, while being carefully controlled with breathtaking precision. With luck, you've had the opportunity to witness and be moved by the live performance of a truly gifted singer, and have felt the goosebumps and tears that come with it. Someone singing well, from the heart, is one of the most captivating experiences that I know. And when I'm the one doing the singing, that experience can be truly transcendent.

At the other end of the spectrum, singing can also be as whimsical as a nursery rhyme, which is more about rhythm, rhyme, story and glee. These factors, truth be told, can be as sacred as

---

The present moment is filled with joy and happiness.

If you are attentive, you will see it.

FROM 'PEACE IS EVERY STEP'
THÍCH NHAT HANH

---

anything else. But my point is that music covers an enormous range, from the ethereal to the ordinary. And for those of us who are dedicated to bringing more awareness to each moment of our lives, we learn to find magic in the ordinary.

Sing for Happiness

Singing is a present-centred art form. By its very nature of engaging the body, heart and mind, singing naturally engenders a sense of mindfulness, waking us up and making us feel alive. We are less likely to be distracted while singing. It certainly happens, of course, like when we're singing along with one of our favourite songs while taking a trip down memory lane. That's part of the magic of music too. But when we are in a room by ourselves, or in a group, getting to know our voices, working on vocal exercises or giving a performance, a sense of presence naturally arises when we're singing.

The more present we are, the more elevated our mood can become. Singing, quite simply, makes us feel good. This is true for us on a subjective level and it's also supported by scientific research.

By releasing neurochemicals dopamine and oxytocin into the brain, singing promotes feelings of well-being, belonging and happiness, while reducing the presence of those chemicals related to stress and anxiety. Singing makes us happy.

So does mindfulness. Similar research supports the idea that we feel better when we are present, momentarily free from the neurotic spaces we are prone to inhabiting as human beings. Worry, busy-ness, stress, insecurity, fear, anxiety, anger, loneliness, all of those normal experiences that are part of our human lives – those thoughts and feelings have a tendency to fall into the background when we sing, and when we are present. Spending more time in those mindful spaces allows us to rest more comfortably into who we really are – relaxed, open and loving. And someone who loves to sing.

Sing for Loving-Kindness

Singing brings about what the Buddhists refer to as *metta*, or loving-kindness – the sincere and altruistic desire for all beings to be happy and free from suffering. The more we sing, the more connected we become with our hearts, with ourselves. And when that occurs, we are naturally more kind, gentle and loving towards each other. So singing doesn't just benefit you, it benefits everyone else too.

That's no joke – try singing every day for a month, then let me know how you're feeling about yourself, and how you're treating others. The results may surprise you.

FINDING YOUR VOICE

◆

If we think of our voices at all, we tend to think of them for speaking
— but using our voices only for speaking is like using the internet
only for email. Singing opens up an entire world of possibilities for
using our voices, offering uncountable avenues for self-expression.

M
Y OWN PERSONAL AND PROFESSIONAL JOURNEYS have
found me adopting a variety of roles, including father,
performing songwriter, school counsellor, music therapist,
play therapist, football coach, university professor and now
author. Much of my work along the way has been with children and adolescents, and I am reminded daily of the necessity
for each of us to feel as though we have a certain level of control over what happens to us; we need to have a voice.

I want to let you in on a little-known and scarcely believed
secret: we are all meant to sing. That's right. Not only *can* you
sing, but you are actually *meant* to. It's good for you on a
number of levels. You came into this world knowing how to
do it, and loving it. If you're among the fortunate, that love of
singing never left you, and it remains a part of your daily life.
But many of us became disconnected from our voices ages ago
or grew self-conscious because of teasing or other external
criticism that was painful enough for us to shut our voices
down. We stopped singing, or maybe we believed the lie that
said we couldn't. That painful story is common, as many of us

have early developmental wounding that affects our creative expression. But as with most things, healing requires us to embrace and accept those places that frighten us, rather than run from them.

In reconnecting with our voices, especially through a mindful lens of heightened awareness, the act of singing itself becomes the antidote to those poisonous thoughts underlying the myth that you couldn't or shouldn't sing. You can, you should, and doing so makes a world of difference.

Let Your Voice Be Heard

For those of us who think of ourselves as singers, it's a rare gift to meet someone else who also sings. Even we 'singers' frequently grow so nervous and shy when it comes to our voices that when we're asked directly if we sing, many of us will make a joke, avert our eyes, blush and mumble some variation of 'sort of'. This is a tragic state of affairs: that for many of us, we have either given up singing altogether, or we continue to sing but do so without fully owning our voices. It's like being half alive.

The cave you fear to enter holds the treasure you seek.

JOSEPH CAMPBELL (1904–87)
AMERICAN EDUCATOR, AUTHOR AND EXPERT ON WORLD MYTHOLOGY

In part, we can thank our recent obsessions with reality television and singing competitions for silencing some of us and shifting our perceptions. By turning the scathing criticism of someone's vocal performance into public entertainment, even fewer of us are willing to let our voices be heard. And fewer of us yet would dare to admit that we love to sing. But this book is one attempt to counteract that mistaken thinking. I envision a time when it's a foregone conclusion that we all sing and dance, as we laugh and breathe. This doesn't mean that every voice is worthy of a recording contract, but everyone can, in fact, sing. And it's important that we do.

No One Can Sing Like You

Wonderful, dynamic, creative you! There has never before in the history of time been another *you*, and there never will be. And you know what? That matters. And while you invariably share a number of things in common with other human beings, your uniqueness is on full display when you open your mouth to sing. Which is part of why it frightens us to do so.

Mindful Tune-up

Go and find your favourite song, turn up the volume and sing along. Pay attention to how you feel while the song is playing and the way that you feel afterwards.

Whether or not we hear it, *everything* has a sound,

a vibration all its own.

FROM 'THE POWER OF SOUND'
JOSHUA LEEDS

Your singing voice is yours alone. It's you — encapsulated in sound. You're important! Now I realize some people may argue that saying everyone is special is just another way of saying that nobody is special. Right? Wrong! Your voice is different from everybody else's, conveying a unique combination of thoughts, feelings, experiences and relationships that have never before existed. All of these aspects of what it means to be you come through in your voice, which is why we can feel so vulnerable when we sing. Our pitchy notes, our cracks, our blemishes, our insecurities — people are likely to hear them when we sing. Then everyone will know that we aren't perfect. Which is what allows them to connect with us in the first place — our vulnerability, our willingness to put ourselves out there and to be heard, even in all of our imperfection. We all know it's frightening to perform in front of others and we respect other people when they do it. We'll discuss live performances and how to deal with nerves in later chapters, but for now, we are celebrating the uniqueness of your voice. No one can sing like you!

Serving Notice

When done well, singing becomes a meditation in auditory form. It arouses our awareness and invigorates our bodies, stimulates our spirit and opens our hearts. And in addition to being something fun and entertaining, we will also discover some ways in which singing is healing, especially with regard to those emotional wounds connected to our creativity. Our voices are sacred, and using them to sing lifts us into our rightful place in the universe – singing along with everything else.

This book will cover a lot of territory, from the constant vibration of every molecule in the universe to the lifting of your soft palate. Along the way, you will be encouraged to *notice* certain things. Notice your breath, notice your body, notice your tone and so on. This is the essence of mindfulness. Being in the present moment, paying close attention to what is happening both internally and externally, without judgement. These are the underpinnings of a mindful way of living and, as we'll explore, mindful living changes everything – and it begins with increasing our sense of awareness. Singing wakes us up, invigorates our body, regulates our nervous system and makes us happy. That is a lot to notice.

The Journey Begins

While the simple act of singing is rather easy, learning to sing properly and with adequate breath support takes practice. Remember to be gentle with yourself as we embark on this journey together. Keeping a sense of play and levity serves us well (nearly always), especially when we're navigating the vulnerable waters in which our creative voices swim. Keeping a journal about your singing is a good idea, too.

Whether you are a professional singer, a shower singer or one of the many people who haven't really sung since child-hood or ever, this book is for you. May it offer avenues for connecting with your voice in new ways, returning you to the present moment, enriching your life, reclaiming that which is your birthright and transforming your voice into its most ethereal form – song.

◆

'Widening Circles'

I live my life in widening circles

that reach out across the world.

I may not complete this last one

but I give myself to it.

I circle around God, around the primordial tower.

I've been circling for thousands of years

and I still don't know: am I a falcon,

a storm, or a great song?

FROM 'BOOK OF HOURS: LOVE POEMS TO GOD'
RAINER MARIA RILKE

CHAPTER ONE

◆

GETTING STARTED

When I try to express my thoughts and
feelings about singing, the first words that come
to mind are positive descriptions — invigorating,
expressive, vital. Yet many among us immediately think
of singing as difficult, frightening or intimidating.
For starters, let's begin by being gentle with ourselves
and the critical parts of our minds that are prone to
judgement. As with any mindful endeavour, our aim
is simply to be present with what is — in this case,
our singing voices, regardless of how we think they
sound. For now, simply singing is enough. Give
yourself permission to sing every day.

Be Here Now

The essence of mindfulness is very simple: be here now. Tune in to this very moment, notice what is happening right now. Take a breath, notice how it feels, take another. Become aware of your thoughts, the energy in your body, directing your attention to the experience you are having in this very moment, the only moment we have. Take another breath. Be here now. Right here. Nowhere else. Not at work, not on that phone call you have to make. Be here. Right now. Tune in. Slow down. Breathe. Notice. This is mindfulness.

WHAT IS MINDFULNESS?

It's something that I can usually sense the moment I meet someone. They're here, plugged in, making contact. They shake my hand and look me in the eye like most people, but there is something else. It's a sense of presence, curiosity and subtle joy. They're mindful.

I WAS RAISED IN A VERY CLOSE-KNIT, loving family who valued self-discipline and striving for success. The family motto was 'work hard and save your money', a method that has served many family members well. It is also a motto that is focused on *doing, accomplishing* and *achieving*. These things have their place, but it was later in life that I got more in touch with *being*, learning to slow down, be still and develop a different type of relationship with myself. That was no easy task, as many of us learn to identify with certain aspects of what we do, what we accomplish, where we work, what we drive and so on. That requires a lot of *doing*. And who are we without those things? Many of us don't know, and some of us don't care to find out. But for those of us who are interested in knowing ourselves on deeper levels, in a more substantive way, an exploration into mindful living offers a pathway.

Mindfulness is an easy concept to understand – be present – and very challenging to practise in a regular, moment-by-moment fashion. Because as soon as we have a simple moment of feeling present, awake and aware, we are suddenly swept away by another thought or emotion. This happens throughout every waking *Mindfulness is an easy concept to understand* moment of our days. New thoughts, new feelings, new and seductive shiny things to grab our attention, often taking us away from the present moment. How long can we go without checking our mobile phones?

Start Somewhere

Learning how to simply *be* and to observe our minds is still a foreign concept to many of us, especially in the Western world. Just sitting still, breathing? I've got things to do! Kids to raise! No time to sit. Maybe later. Yeah, right.

To this end, I say start *somewhere*. Sit still for ten seconds. Two breaths. Then thirty seconds, a minute. Build up to twenty minutes if you're able. Just simple, still, quiet breathing for twenty minutes a day. There is a vast and growing body of evidence supporting a long list of benefits tied to meditation, including less stress and more happiness. Just like singing. It sounds simple, right? Sitting quietly for twenty minutes a day? But for many of us, especially beginners, we find those twenty minutes can feel excruciatingly tedious, boring and never-ending. Keep trying, do what you can. We all have to start somewhere, and even a few minutes a day of mindful presence is far better than no time spent at all.

Whether you are new to the concept of mindfulness or have been practising it for years, the ideas in the book are straightforward, in part because mindfulness and singing have a natural affinity for one another. It's not just that we are encouraged to be present in order to sing well; the act of singing itself engenders a sense of presence. Singing wakes us up, brings us into the now, vibrating within and without our bodies, and it is one activity that offers a beautiful interplay between *doing* and *being*.

Learning to Be

After a mostly rather happy childhood spent near Seattle, Washington, I found myself ready for a change of scenery following my high-school graduation. I had been accepted to my first choice of colleges, and moved down the West Coast to enrol at the University of California, Berkeley, across the bay from San Francisco.

Berkeley is a city known for its esteemed university, its famously liberal politics and its colourful diversity. A city with its own rhythm, Berkeley has an electric vibe that hums with an undercurrent of tension, creativity and unrest. I still found it to be quite safe, although my grandmother clutched her handbag a bit more tightly while we traversed the city streets. With its history of political turmoil, the city is a unique cauldron that fosters immense creativity, where the boundaries of personal expression are commonly pushed, if not ignored altogether.

In my formative years, I learned early on that I had a knack for verbal sparring, especially with my mother. I revelled in, and seemed to be naturally good at, arguing. When I had once again backed my mother into a verbal corner, she would play-fully relent, adding that I should some day become a lawyer.

And indeed, when I first attended Berkeley I had clear plans to become an attorney. But the more I learned about that path, the less fulfilling I thought it would be in the long run. As much as I knew that I needed to pursue a career that was intellectually challenging, I was also aware that I would thrive when I could work closely with others. Relationships had always been at the heart of what mattered most to me, and I had always been curious to hear other people's stories.

Change of Plan

While working my way through my first academic year at the university, I discovered an opportunity to follow these natural curiosities in my first psychology class. I was quickly enthralled to learn about the brain, theories of personality and trauma, defence mechanisms and vulnerability. I didn't fully realize it at the time, but enrolling in that psychology course set my life's path for the next several decades.

One of the many things that encouraged me to major in psychology was that it was a rather broad topic, offering a very wide array of possibilities for continued areas of focus. While perusing the prospectus during my second year, I was particularly drawn to a course on 'Buddhist Psychology'. I'm not sure why, truth be told. I knew very little about Buddhism at the time, but had always been curious.

I was raised in a fairly conservative Christian household, and will be forever grateful for the strong foundation, close family ties and spiritual connection my upbringing afforded me. At the same time, my insatiable curiosity about life, the afterlife and my own inner life extended in every direction, and I was desperate to explore. So there I was, a wide-eyed college student at a vibrant university, with unfettered access to some of the world's top scholars in areas of psychology, religion, philosophy, sociology and more. I was in heaven. Or maybe not heaven exactly, because this class was Buddhist Psychology, and I was not sure they believed in heaven.

DISCOVERING MEDITATION

◆

The basic form is simple: sit still, breathe, focus the mind on the breathing. That's it. Easy enough. Until we have a thought. And another. And we follow them, because they're so important. Or not. Come back to the breath. Be here now. Only here.

Are You an Efficient Cheetah?

As I learned how to meditate, I realized how busy my mind usually stayed, and that having a *thought* about being present is very different from actually *being present*. I slowly became more aware of the spaces in between my thoughts, and I was able to rest there for longer periods of time. Learning to be. Not do. Just be. I truly had never heard of such a thing.

I came by this honestly, though, as my mother is much the same way, busy and productive, perpetually in motion. Our family took a light-hearted personality quiz that determined your particular personality animal. I am the Communicating Elephant, and my mother is the Efficient Cheetah. Funny how accurate a simple personality quiz can be.

I slowly became more aware of the spaces in between my thoughts, and I was able to rest there for longer periods of time

Learning to Meditate

In our first class, the instructor walked us through a basic introduction to meditation. There were nearly one hundred students in the lecture hall, each of us seated and facing forward.

Close your eyes, *she instructed*, and place your attention on your breath as it flows past your nostrils. As you breathe in, say silently to yourself 'breathing in'. As you are exhaling, say to yourself 'breathing out'. Eventually we let go of the words, and were instructed to simply observe our breath. One after the other. And again. As thoughts arise and your mind wanders, gently return to your breath, again and again.

OK, I can do this, I thought. It seems easy enough. I close my eyes, take a few deep breaths, and try to focus on the sensation of the air flowing past my nostrils. Not so hard, I think. I can totally do it. Yes. See? I just did it! I'm totally focused on that sensation. I wonder if everyone else can do it like this? Maybe this guy next to me. I wonder what his name is ... wait ... whoops ... breathing, nostrils, being present. Right. I'm back. Breathing in. Breathing out. I got this. Breathing. Breathing. Easy. Is it always so easy? Maybe I'm just a natural. And ... ah! That was thinking. Come back to breathing. This is harder than I thought.

I return to the breath. More thoughts intrude. I follow them for a while, then I catch myself. Then I grow bored again. I straighten my spine, open up my chest as instructed and then return my attention to my breath. But that only lasts for a moment or two. This is so boring. I cannot imagine people choosing to do this for twenty minutes a day. We've got to be getting close to our time, right? No? It's only been four minutes?! You have got to be kidding! I can do this. I think. This is hard.

Learning to sit and do nothing? Just breathe? Well, in addition to being boring, that was just being lazy. Being idle seemed to fly in the face of everything I thought I was meant to be, or do. But then that was the real problem, right there. I knew how to *do*. Just tell me what to do, and I can do it! In fact, I'll do it better than it's ever been done. That's how good I am at doing. But what I really didn't know how to do was to *be*. I didn't want to just sit and be. I didn't know how, and I didn't feel naturally good at it. Therefore, I shouldn't have to do it, right?

But I did it anyway, just like they showed me, and I started to notice things. Subtle things about myself and my thinking. Like how my thoughts tended to follow certain patterns, and my emotional world followed suit. And how I tended to tell myself the same story about some person or some aspect of my life, repeating the same tired narrative and reinforcing my version of the truth. How we love to be right.

EXERCISE

THE SQUARE BREATH

The square breath is a very accessible tool designed to be used anywhere and everywhere, in moments of calm as well as agitation. It has four simple parts: breathe in, hold for a moment, breathe out, hold for a moment. Repeat. It's a very effective way to take a pause, and can be a vital resource in moments of irritability.

Tuning in to Life

The more I meditated, the more tuned in I became to other areas of my life where I naturally felt more present. Physical and pleasurable activities were usually high on this list, of course, such as playing sports, and other sensory pleasures like showering and sex. But even simple things like sweeping or washing the dishes took on another dimension. This is presence, this is mindfulness, this is simply becoming aware. Moment by moment, breath by breath, tuning in to now.

I also started noticing that the longer I was able to rest in those expansive spaces in between thoughts, the better I felt. It turns out that simply *being* actually feels really good. Which is understandable when we remember that who we actually are is present, loving, open – the rest of it is just window dressing and the result of relational wounds. When we return to this simple place again, one breath at a time, and when we bring that sense of presence into the other areas of our lives, we naturally begin to feel better. Then we add in the singing, and life begins to reveal all sorts of spectacular possibilities.

Mindful Tune-up

Before you begin singing, take a moment to become present. Feel your feet standing on the ground or your buttocks sitting on the chair, breathe.

THE BENEFITS OF MINDFUL SINGING

◆

Any singing is healthy, leaving us feeling better than before —
but when combined with the art of mindfulness, singing can become
transformative. Mindful singing tunes us in, wakes us up and
expresses our emotions in ways that leave us feeling more open,
connected and joyful. Who doesn't want that?

SINGING WAKES UP OUR BODIES. By activating the many
systems involved in producing vocal sound, the act of
singing itself engages muscles, moves energy, burns calories,
increases oxygen to the brain and stimulates
a variety of feel-good hormones, all of *Singing is*
which leaves us feeling alive, alert, awake, *a meditation*
expansive and present. Numerous studies *in sound*
have shown that singing reduces symptoms
of anxiety, depression and high blood pressure, while increasing self-esteem, alertness and a general sense of well-being.
Singing is powerful medicine.

So is practising mindfulness. In fact, many studies show the
same type of benefits with meditation and other mindfulness
practices as with singing: reduced stress, a greater sense of
joy. The combination of the two, mindful singing, recognizes
that singing is a meditation in sound, a sacred practice of
using our voices to bring us in to the present and to connect
us with everything else.

Changing Your Lived Experience

As you practise each of the exercises in this book, use them as opportunities to create more space around you, to become more aware of the sensations in your body, noticing how your awareness of these same sensations throughout your day can change your lived experience.

Take, for example, the experience of anger. When it gets the better of me, I raise my voice, my jaw grows tight and my stomach is knotted with tension. In a more mindful moment, however, I strive to take a breath, then another. I can still feel the tension in my stomach and jaw, I still feel angry, but I'm also able to breathe while I'm observing these sensations. I don't need to push them away, though they're admittedly uncomfortable. As I continue to breathe, these sensations eventually fade, allowing me to collect myself before I have uttered a single word.

Wouldn't it be nice if we could always respond in this manner, allowing ourselves a pause in between the triggering event and our response to it? The truth is, you can learn to respond in this way, and repeatedly, with a little practice. And mindful singing can help.

Positive Emotions

As the Buddhist Psychology class progressed, we ventured into the realm of emotions, discussing two different viewpoints. One of these focused on creating happiness by doing (or buying) things that made us happy, at least temporarily, while the other view sought to reduce or remove those things that made us unhappy. Like stress and tension.

The discussion returned to meditation, and how the experience of watching the mind was a metaphor for the transient nature of life. Things and people come and go like thoughts. Let's relax our grip a little, shifting our relationship with these things by allowing them to be what they are instead of forcing them to be what we want. The same is true for our emotions. They, too, will come and go, like thunderclouds. Surfing those emotional waves involves a gentle returning to the breath and the now. The more that we experienced being present, the more a sense of well-being seemed to arise.

I realize this may sound a bit naive, but by using our breath or our singing voice to return to the present, we can effectively remove stress and neurosis. It's not like we can sing

---

Back to Loving-Kindness

Positive emotions come about when we return to who we really are, the loving and compassionate beings we all become when the stress and fear are removed. Ever notice how nice and happy people tend to be when they're on holiday? A daily meditation helps us remember who we really are, returning us again and again to a state of loving-kindness.

EXERCISE

BASIC BREATH

Sit quietly, follow your breath with thoughts of 'breathing in ... breathing out ...'. Let your mind and body become in sync. Then when you're ready, sing a long *Ahhh* sound, paying attention to the moment the body engages the breath and the vocal chords engage to create your tone. Notice the moment your breath becomes your voice, feel the vibrations it creates throughout your body.

---

away the real-world stresses that come with being human. But in a way, we can, and we do. Not only do we move ourselves into more positive emotional states when we sing with presence, but the vibrations of music also leave us better equipped to deal with stresses long after we're done singing.

The idea is laughably simple. The more I let my mind become occupied with the future, the more likely I am to become anxious, increasing my stress. In contrast, the more my mind drifts into the past, the more likely I am to become mired in guilt and regret. The third option – maintaining an awareness in the present – is optimal. We learn that emotions appear like thunderclouds, here one minute and gone the next. We become less attached to any one emotional state of being, and learn how to relax. We are not the thunderclouds. They pass through. We are basic awareness. We are the sky.

THE SOUND OF LIFE

*The Hindu saying 'Nada Brahma' — from the Sanskrit word nada,
which means sound, and Brahma, the Hindu name for God — is often
translated as 'God is Sound' or 'The World is Sound'. Everything is
singing. And it turns out that this matters. Because these voices, and
the sound they produce, make a measurable difference in our world.*

EVEN THOUGH AS HUMAN BEINGS we feel somewhat 'stuck'
in the normal routine of life, the truth is that every single
thing in the universe is in motion, all of the time. Stop and let
that sink in for a moment. Ha! Stop. You can't stop. Your heart
still beats, your breath still moves. Your mind as well. This
constant motion is true on the subatomic level for everything,
from the bark on the tree to the ceramic in your coffee cup.
Everything is vibrating. You may not see it or feel it, but it's
true. And vibration creates sound waves. So even though you
can't hear it, everything in the universe is singing.

If only we could hear the full creation of the sound,

The clouds and grasses singing, subtle symphonies surround,

The magic of magnificence has left us little choice,

Our sacred contribution is the sharing of our voice.

'IF ONLY WE COULD HEAR'
JEREMY DION

There is another alphabet, whispering from every leaf,

singing from every river, shimmering from every sky.

FROM 'FORGOTTEN HOME'
DEJAN STOJANOVIC

While our limited human senses clearly lack the fine tuning required to hear all of these cosmic waves, that doesn't stop them from existing. Everything around us is singing in the background, just waiting for us to join in. Our voices connect us with the rest of the natural world, and we honour that sacred connection most when we use them to sing. In fact, when we spend more time singing, we find ourselves feeling more connected in general – with ourselves, with other people and with the natural world – and this usually leaves us feeling better.

Fine-Tuning Our Perception

Sadly, as incredible as our human brains are, we hear only a very small slice of this cosmic music. Estimates vary, but the human ear is typically able to hear less than one per cent of the acoustic spectrum. One per cent! That means 99 per cent of this cosmic singing is completely wasted on us. So sad. And just in case you think our ears are special in their limited regard, our eyes are no better. We typically perceive less than one per cent of the existing electromagnetic spectrum, too.

Imagine, for a moment, if our perceptions were more developed. That in addition to hearing the daily sounds of life – traffic, voices, ringing telephones – we could also hear the magnificent symphony that included singing grasses, humming trees and whistling clouds. Or that we could hear the subtle distinction in the emotional sound someone was making as their mood shifted during conversation. Some of these things we feel anyway, some of us more than others. Perception is a subtle thing and the more present we are, the more aware we become, the more we perceive. How might the dance of relationships be different if we became more finely tuned instruments, capable of perceiving the subtle energetic shifts in ourselves and others? How can mindful singing help us to become more finely tuned instruments?

Perpetual Flux

With everything constantly vibrating, we are simultaneously emitting and receiving vibrations as well, leaving us in a perpetual state of emotional and psychological flux. We inherently know this to be true, as our emotional world is affected by the shifting dynamic of each passing moment. The song playing in the background changes, and my mood changes with it. The weather shifts, and my emotional reality follows suit. I receive

Perception is a subtle thing and the more present we are, the more aware we become

that email I'd been waiting for, and I'm elated. Then I read it, it's bad news, and I'm dejected. So it goes, the inherent drama that is largely inseparable from the human condition. The more present we become, the more mindfully we surf these waves, the less attached we become to any one emotion. It becomes easier to remember that this intense moment we're having is as transient as any other. We breathe, allowing the feeling to move through, replaced by another.

It's often helpful to shift our vibrations in a purposeful manner, like going jogging to alleviate stress, or practising the square breath to come back to ourselves. Or when we play a particular song to help shift our current mood and we sing, we are consciously changing our own internal vibrations. We can change how we feel. Other times we are more at the mercy of our surroundings, seemingly helpless to impact change. But we're now developing at least one vital tool that will never leave us as long as we're still drawing breath: our singing voices.

Taking Responsibility

Given the perpetual flux of everything within and around us, it becomes imperative that we take responsibility for our own realities and the experiences we are having. We like to blame others for our reactions with statements such as, 'But you made me so cross!' As if I am helpless to alter my response. Granted, we've all been in situations where our emotions got

EXERCISE

THE MORNING HUM

After getting out of bed but before you've got too far in your morning routine, find a quiet place to sit or stand. With your eyes and lips closed, inhale slowly. On the exhale, hum a single long note (*Mmmmm*), which lasts as long as your breath does. Feel the vibrations emanating from your lips and face. Do the same thing with your next breath, but this time choose a note that is higher or lower in pitch than the first one. Notice any differences in the location and intensity of the vibrations that you feel as you try humming different notes.

Keep doing this for several breaths. Explore both the high and low ends of your vocal register. Then begin varying your pitch – start humming one note, and switch notes mid-breath. Sing two notes in one long breath. Then three. Find your own melody, or sing a melody that is familiar to you. Follow your inner wisdom. Keep this up for several minutes or more, allowing your body to move and sway as the music moves through you. Try humming loudly, and more softly, noticing the differences in vibrations through your body.

As you feel ready to close this mindful exercise, keep your eyes closed for a moment after you've finished humming. Breathe. Notice the vital life force coursing through your body. Allow a subtle smile to form on your face. As you transition from this moment into the rest of your morning, see if you can carry this feeling with you throughout your day. Keep buzzing.

the better of us, and we said or did that unkind thing in response to our emotional state. But we can do better. We can slow down, tune in and work with our emotions in healthy ways. Singing can help with this, starting with the vibrational effect in has on our bodies and minds.

Our voices offer an easy and effective way to shift our vibrations, and can be used daily in a variety of helpful ways. Quieten the inner critic that judges your singing or subtly convinces you not to, and decide that you're worth it. Try starting out by singing each morning for a week, and see what kind of impact it has on your day.

Sound Affects Form

One reason singing makes such an impact on our sense of well-being has to do with the actual vibrations themselves. Our voices are more powerful than you think, and we can use them to shift our moods, open up our hearts and bring us repeatedly into the present moment. We already know that music affects how we feel, as our favourite songs can move our bodies and stir our emotions like nothing else. But we're talking about the actual sound waves here, and how they effect changes in matter.

Quieten the inner critic that judges your singing or subtly convinces you not to, and decide that you're worth it

---

Everything is sound. Sound takes random particles
and turns it into stunning form.

FROM 'CYMATICS: A STUDY OF WAVE PHENOMENA AND VIBRATION'
HANS JENNY

It has been shown that even common houseplants respond to sound waves, turning towards classical music and away from hard rock, for example. In other research, scientists played the recorded sound of a caterpillar feasting on leaves to a group of plants, which responded to the threatening sound by producing defensive chemicals. Plants can listen, and respond to what they hear. For further explanation of the science behind the impact of sound waves, we are going to rewind the clock back to eighteenth-century Germany.

Organized by Sound

Physicist and musician Ernst Chladni set out to verify what shamans and sages have known for centuries: sound waves affect matter. Often referred to as the 'father of acoustics', Chladni invented a technique to explore and explain the effect of sound and vibration. By drawing his violin bow across the edge of a metal sheet that had been covered with sand, he found that the sound waves organized the grains of sand into different visual patterns. The higher the frequency of the sound waves, the more complex the visual pattern became, illustrating the 'nodal lines' where the surface remained still, while other parts of the metal vibrated. The visual patterns became known around the world, now visually represented and referred to as 'Chladni figures', and these are still used today in the construction of a number of acoustic musical instruments.

Nearly 200 years later, Swiss doctor Hans Jenny took this research a step further, capturing a series of stunning images of the geometric patterns created by different sound waves.

Jenny also noticed that the arrangement of the molecules into patterns tended to fall apart when the sound waves stopped. In essence, Jenny found that sound not only affects form, organizing it into complex patterns, but it also sustains those shapes only as long as the music lasts. This idea may hold true for humans as well, as we too seem to fall apart if our music stops.

Chladni and Dr Jenny have hit upon something profound, and the implications of these discoveries are immense in their scope. Because if sound can affect substance, how might music affect the thirty-seven trillion cells in our bodies? How can we harness the power of sound and singing to reach optimal health? And how important is singing to overall well-being?

TUNING IN

◆

Many sacred traditions around the globe share a sense of quiet. A time for reflection, prayer, meditation, reverence, gratitude, love; it's all made of the same expansive qualities of the Divine. It's what we are all made of, and it's that to which we all return when we become present.

THERE'S A PART OF US THAT ALWAYS REMEMBERS who we are, and is ready to remind us at a moment's notice. But the only way we can hear it is by growing quiet and tuning in. It's all too easy to forget to listen, because most of the time that inner voice sings pretty softly, whispers even, and it's much easier to become caught up in all of the noise surrounding us. That's more true today than ever before, as we are all constantly bombarded by news alerts, emails, phone calls, texts, things to do, things to say, places to go and people to pay. And there's not enough time. There's never enough time! All of it's important, we can't drop the ball, we've just got to somehow come up with it all. Or so we tell ourselves. Repeatedly.

Buddhists have a phrase I resonate with: don't believe everything you think. We can actually escape from the rat race, from living our lives consumed with *doing*, and wearing our exhaustion like a merit badge. There is another way. A more centred, present, mindful way of living. It has to do with being, with singing and with noticing.

EXERCISE

YOUR TOP TEN

With pen and paper, write down your top ten favourite songs. Don't overthink it, just write the first ten that come to mind. Then learn to sing along with each of those songs. If you don't already have recordings, go and find them online. After learning the melody lines to each song, try singing the background harmonies if you're able to hear them. As for discovering new music, there are a variety of online resources and apps that generate a list of musicians based upon those you already like. Go exploring.

The Art of Noticing

So the good news is, the more you look, the more you see. The bad news happens to be the same. As we become more mindful, we start noticing all sorts of things that we didn't see before. The busy-ness of our minds, the tension that we hold in our bodies, and the fickle nature of our emotions – that's a lot to keep track of. As we tune in to what's happening in the moment, we become more acutely aware that feelings such as sadness and anger are alive within us as sensations in our bodies, and we can use our bodies to work with those feelings and overcome them. Noticing, paying attention, taking in a breath, tuning in, these things are all essential components to a mindful life. When we then add singing from this self-aware posture, the effects can be profound.

At a retreat centre in France, a large bell tolls periodically throughout the day in the heart of the small village. Whenever people hear the bell, they pause whatever it was they were doing, and tune in to whatever is happening within and around them, taking a few mindful breaths before going about their day. It is incumbent upon each of us to come up with our own 'bells' throughout our day – those things that give us reason to pause, tune in and allow a moment of reflection without needing to change anything. This is the art of mindfulness.

Like What You See?

There is a price to pay, as I mentioned before, in that we don't always like what we see once we start looking. Each of us is likely to observe aspects of ourselves, our thinking, our actions and our personalities that we're not especially proud of, parts of us we'd rather keep hidden. But the more we look, the more we realize that one vital aspect to creating happiness lies in practising gratitude and repeated, gentle acceptance. The more we are able to accept ourselves and others, the less attached we become to the way things need to be and the more we can learn to relax into the way things are.

Feelings are just visitors, let them come and go.

MOOJI
JAMAICAN SPIRITUAL TEACHER

We have more possibilities available in each

moment than we realize.

THÍCH NHẠT HANH
VIETNAMESE BUDDHIST MONK, AUTHOR AND PEACE ACTIVIST

We can loosen our grip on life, and this is the lesson we remember repeatedly through mindful living. Thoughts and feelings, like thunderclouds, pass through. Like everything.

The more we remember this when we sing, the better we'll do. Simply practise the art of noticing. The feelings we have while singing – from the bliss to the terror and everything in between – are all part of the package. We don't let the scary emotions shut us down, any more than we become attached to the pleasurable ones. Everything is in motion, all of the time. So we carry on noticing, breathing and singing.

Gut Instinct

I'm sure you are aware that while many among us consider ourselves to be emotional beings, others are much less so. My mother cries during touching television commercials, while her stoic husband sits stonily (although lovingly) beside her. I know some people who never have a feeling without sharing it, and others who scarcely know that what they are having is a feeling. Even for those of us who feel deeply, many lack the ability to articulate these nebulous emotional landscapes.

One thing I have found to be helpful is simply learning to notice the sensations in the body, which has wisdom far beyond anything we can pretend to comprehend. The body remembers on a cellular level, and stores memories in ways we don't yet understand. But my experience has taught me that my body's wisdom, and its intuitive, empathic feeling sensors, can frequently be trusted to steer me in the right direction. My intuition, or *gut instinct,* keeps me on a positive course far more often than not, as long as I remember to tune in and listen. And I am not unique in this regard – we all have an internal compass that seems to know more than our head does, but many of us forget to listen.

So let's tune in and start noticing and listening everywhere we go. The more we listen, the more we hear. The more we look, the more we see. The more we breathe, the more options we have available to us.

Mindful Tune-up

Play a familiar song, sing along, experience that surge of joy that accompanies the vibrations and emotional sensations that come along with singing to, let alone simply listening to, one of your favourite songs.

CHAPTER TWO

BREATH & BODY, THE MAKING OF A VOICE

More dynamic than a fingerprint, yet just as singular and identifiable. Our voices are unique, capable of producing an astounding array of tones and conveying a dizzying spectrum of emotion and meaning. Carrying our words, our songs and our stories, our voices tell the world who we are and how we are doing in this very moment. It is through our voices that we give ourselves permission to say yes and no, to shout, to whisper, to laugh, to sob, to speak and to sing. Most of all, let our voices sing.

THE MAKING OF A VOICE

◆

Relationships thrive upon connection, presence and a healthy dose
of curiosity. We need to get better acquainted. As we learn to deepen
our relationship with our voices, let's get to know them from the
ground up, so we can fully appreciate their magnificence.

ANYONE COURAGEOUS ENOUGH TO SING has a slightly
different story about their voice. All of those subjective
things are important aspects to the tale – when did we start
singing? What feedback did we receive? Were we surrounded
by others singing, or did we come to it on our own? Who
were our musical influences? Do we like our voices? Who do
we wish we sounded like? Each of us has a unique answer to
these questions, and the matrix of our responses has an impact
on our relationship with our voices. For now, let's distil the
discussion down to the basics in the hope of understanding
exactly what is required to sing.

When it comes to making a voice, the basic three-part
recipe includes the lungs, the larynx and the articulators (the
tongue, lips, etc). Air makes the vocal chords vibrate, and the
muscles in the larynx stretch and shorten the smooth folds of
muscle to articulate pulses of air, forming the basis of words
and phrases. These vocal folds are located in the larynx (voice
box), and they comprise two bands of smooth muscle tissue,
which snap closed when we swallow and vacillate between

open and closed positions when we speak. When we breathe gently, these same bands of tissue relax to an open posture, allowing air to pass through unencumbered.

As we prepare to speak, our brains coordinate a series of complex movements in the vocal chords while simultaneously modulating the amount of air flowing from the lungs. It is the movement of the air passing through the vocal chords that produces vibration and sound, but from there the quality of the sound produced varies dramatically.

Work With What You Have

Just as we get wildly different outcomes by singing in an empty and cavernous gymnasium versus singing in a carpeted bedroom, the quality of the sound depends greatly on the space in which the sound waves are produced. This is as true for external spaces (gymnasiums versus bedrooms) as it is for the internal spaces of our throat, nose, mouth and chest. In fact, our entire bodies act as an instrument when we sing. They vibrate and resonate with sound, and the more we learn how to sing with the whole body, the more resonant our instrument becomes.

In the same way in which a string instrument's sound is affected by its size, shape and the type of wood used in the construction, our singing voices also take on their own unique character based on, in part, the particularities of the many resonating chambers in our bodies. Even small variations in the size and shape of these internal structures alters the shape of the sound we create when we sing, making our singing voices sound as varied as our facial features appear.

The simple beauty of singing is that even though some people will appear to have been given more talent than us in the singing department, each of us can work with what we've been given. Singing is for everyone, and with a few simple tips we can improve our tone, stamina and confidence.

It's All About the Breath

This is a pretty good prescription for life, actually – it's all about the breath. The more we consciously breathe, the more aware we become, the more options we have available to us, the less reactive we are. It's that simple. As we follow the rhythm of our breathing and tune in to the nuances of the world in the present moment, we slow down, we notice and we settle. Our simple, conscious breath is an ever-present, gentle reminder to be here now in this very moment, which is the only one we have.

One of the fascinating aspects of the breath is that unlike many bodily functions, it is both automatic and controllable. It is governed by our autonomic nervous system, the one that functions in the background, keeping us alive without us 'doing' anything about it. Yet we can, in any waking moment we choose, take control of the breath and make it do what we want, within reason. We can stop it, start it and control it for

EXERCISE

CREATING SPACE

Sing *La la laaaa* and notice how the tongue lies flat and relaxed. Now sing *E E E eeeeee* and feel the tongue rise at the edges to create the sound, restricting the tone. When singing an *Eeee* sound, try opening the mouth slightly and tucking the chin, creating a little more space in your mouth. Sometimes, shifting the jaw forward slightly and lifting the soft palate (see page 60 for more on the soft palate), creates more space in the sound chamber, enhancing the tone. With your chin slightly tucked, sing another *Ee* sound and imagine the voice travelling up the back of your neck and shooting over the top of your head. This image can help lift the soft palate on the roof of your mouth.

speaking and singing. We can also learn to sing with controlled precision, carefully modulating the volume and tone, easing in and out of notes. It takes a lot of practice, but these are things any aspiring singer can learn to do.

Proper breathing provides the fuel for the voice, and no serious discussion about proper singing mechanics can begin anywhere else. Many vocal students have been taught about 'diaphragmatic breathing' or 'belly breathing' as the proper techniques for singing. If I were being pedantic, I would point out that we don't technically control the diaphragm, we control the intercostals and other abdominal muscles connected

Breath Support

Vocal instructors teach their pupils to sing correctly by emphasizing 'breath support'. The idea behind proper breathing technique is that we learn not only to control the breath and the rate at which we expel air while singing, but also to use more of our body in the entire process, supporting the tone with our core. The strength of our voice comes from the core muscles of our abdomen and back, and we learn to connect those larger muscle groups with the smaller muscles in the throat.

After gathering a breath to sing, proper technique involves gently engaging the abdominal muscles involved in breathing (all thirty-six of them) while singing, supporting the tone coming from your mouth with the strength of your belly, ribs, buttocks, back, legs, feet, chest, heart, head, all of you. The core muscles of your abs and back in particular, should be engaged when you're singing. But here's the trick: we don't want to over-tighten them, such as we might when doing a crunch-type sit-up. That holds too much tension, which risks putting strain on the vocal chords, restricting our tone.

As with most things, we're striving for balance here. We don't want to overdo it by tightening our stomach muscles to the point of straining them. But we also don't want to let our core muscles become flaccid, which can often encourage the singer to 'push' and leads to straining of the muscles in the neck and throat. Instead, we're aiming for our core muscles to be stable, not rigid.

The word *support* is helpful here. The core muscles *support* the voice, leaving the muscles surrounding our vocal chords more relaxed. You should aim for a supportive and engaged core and a relaxed throat.

to the diaphragm. But since I'm not being pedantic, and since 'diaphragmatic' and 'belly' breathing are both common terms in singing circles, we do need to become familiar with them. But as well as these terms, I find it more helpful to talk about 'breath support' (see opposite page).

DEFINING TERMS

Our entire body becomes the instrument when we sing, each of our cells alive and vibrating with the sound of our voices. However, a few particularly resonant areas deserve our attention, as they play a major role in shaping the character of our tone.

AS WE GO ON TO DISCUSS DIFFERENT vocal registers and resonators, let's be clear about our definitions. We will highlight three different vocal registers, those areas of the body where the sound feels like it is concentrated the most (the chest voice, the middle voice and the head voice), and three different resonating structures (the chest, the palate and the mask).

Each of these areas is likely to be engaged and vibrating any time we are singing, but we can create markedly different tones by consciously choosing which areas of the body are primarily engaged when we sing. The same note can be sung in different ways, depending upon the effect we're seeking to create, so let's get to know our voices.

Piano Voice

Imagine you are standing before a piano, each key representing a note your voice is capable of singing. Each of our pianos is a little different; some have rarely, if ever, been played. Some are shiny and new, others are cracked and dusty, but still capable. The tone has character. Most of the pianos have a few keys broken, missing or out of tune, and none of the notes at the high end or the low end work any more. Let's get to know your piano. It may be in need of a tune-up.

Your Vocal Range in Registers

The entirety of your vocal range (from the lowest to the highest notes you are able to sing) is broken up into what are known as vocal registers. While the exact number of vocal registers is a subject of debate among vocal instructors, the most common paradigm refers to three main ones: the chest voice, the middle voice and the head voice.

Chest Voice

The lowest end of our vocal range is called the chest voice. This is the voice that most of us use for speaking, and its sound is full, deep and resonant; the vocal chords are more open. The vibrations we feel when singing (or speaking) with the chest voice are usually felt below the vocal chords, in the area of our upper chest and around the heart. The sound produced with the chest voice feels like it comes straight out of the mouth, without affecting the soft palate or the mask.

Middle Voice

Above the chest voice is the range known as the middle voice, a register that some vocal instructors eschew. I experience the middle voice as the perfect blend between the lower (chest) voice and the upper (head) voice. When using the middle voice, the vocal chords are partially closed, compared with the more open position of the chest voice. The middle voice is full of resonance, vibrating both the lower resonators of the upper chest and the higher resonators of the upper palate and mask. The middle voice is the register that is most commonly used by commercially successful singers, those who grace our radio waves and movie soundtracks.

EXERCISE

GOOD VIBRATIONS

Sing a nice, low *Ahhhh* sound towards the bottom end of your vocal range. Notice the vibrations in your chest, and also note the relaxed muscles around the throat and larynx. It's as though the sound is produced in the chest and needs no other structural engagement.

Head Voice

When we have reached the upper limits of the middle voice, we zip up the vocal chords even further, moving into the range of the head voice. The head voice tends to resonate with the uppermost registers, those in the hard palate and mask. The notes sung with the head voice vibrate the spaces more in the skull than the neck or chest.

Men Only

In addition to the head voice, men also have the higher falsetto range, and I personally have appreciated the recent trend in popular music of more male vocalists exploring their falsetto range. Stretching into those upper reaches of the vocal range gives men access to what is otherwise a ladies-only club, and those higher notes resonate in ways that are hauntingly beautiful, especially within the context of also having access to the deeper, more resonant end of the vocal range.

Three Resonators

Now that we understand the three types of vocal registers, let's explore the three types of resonators – those vibrating areas of the body that carry the sound waves within us and outside of us. Different areas of the body resonate more than others when we sing, but there are three main areas to think about when paying attention to the vibrations we are creating with our voices.

EXERCISE

THREE BY THREE

To experience the different vibrations of the three registers, start by singing a low *Ah* sound in your chest voice. Notice those deep vibrations in the chest. Then continue with the same breath, rising a bit in pitch (to your middle voice) and now singing the *I* vowel sound. Notice how moving from the open *Ah* vowel sound to the *I* sound requires you to close your mouth slightly. The tone begins to shift forward from the *Ah* falling on the back of your soft palate to the *I* falling in the middle. Continue singing by next switching to a more closed vowel sound, an *Eee* sound, which requires a further closing of the mouth. Let the *Eee* sound rise in pitch as well, now accessing the head voice register. So we sang in three different registers, three different vowel sounds. Repeat this exercise, shifting your awareness to your back and follow the changing vibrations as you elevate the tone and close the vowel.

The Chest

An obvious area of the body that becomes consumed with vibration when we sing is the chest. Place your hand over your heart when you sing, particularly when you sing lower in your vocal range, and notice the changes in vibration as you climb higher with the notes you're singing. The resonators in our chest vibrate the most when we're singing in the lower end of our vocal range, and they vibrate less as we climb the sonic ladder into the middle and upper ranges of our voice. Hitting the low notes sends vibrations into our chest, ribs, back, shoulders and, if we are paying close enough attention, the entire body.

This is a key component to mindful singing – tuning in to the body and noticing these vibrations and the constantly shifting energy that accompanies our singing. Each moment is new, and with every phrase we sing we are coming home to ourselves, to the present moment and to the now. In this way

---

EXERCISE

RAISING THE SOFT PALATE

For this exercise, you will need a flashlight and a mirror. Standing in front of the mirror, shine your light into the back of your throat as you first sing the word *Sung*. Notice how the tongue and the palate join together to create the *ung* sound at the end of the word. This is your soft palate in a relaxed, lowered position. With your next breath, transition from singing the word 'Sung' to *Ah* and notice the lifting of the soft palate as the transition is made. The jaw lowers slightly as well, but try to direct your attention to the roof of your mouth and the gentle lifting towards the back of the throat. If, after this exercise, you are still unable to move your soft palate, try yawning. Raising the soft palate to create a spacious resonance chamber is essential to correct singing, so keep practising until you can feel the difference and are controlling your soft palate on demand.

---

our bodies and our singing voices keep returning us to the present again and again, and we can use these resonators to wake us up. Follow the vibrations.

The Palate

A second resonator to become aware of is the palate – this is the roof of your mouth, with your *hard palate* comprising the area closer to your teeth, and the *soft palate* more towards the centre and back of your throat. When singing correctly, the soft palate is gently raised to afford a more spacious resonating chamber. The opposite – lowering the soft palate while speaking or singing – leads to a more 'nasal' or flat-sounding voice without much resonance. Raise the soft palate while singing, it can make a noticeable difference in the tone we create.

Our singing voices return us to the present

The Mask

A third and final resonating area that deserves our attention is the mask. 'Singing into the mask' is a phrase commonly used by vocal coaches, and they are referring to the projection of sound into our upper resonators – those in our faces and heads. Visualize the top row of your teeth, and imagine sending the sound at the root of your upper incisors. This image will help project the sound. 'Sing to the person in the back of the room,' my vocal instructor used to say.

EXERCISE

FEELING THE MASK

Sing the *Mm* sound, and pay particular attention to the vibrations you experience in the lips, mouth, nose and throat. Now switch to singing the *N* sound, followed by the *V* sound. Now modulate the sound by switching back and forth between singing an *Mm* sound and a *Ma* sound. Notice the decrease in the vibration of the mask when we sing a more open vowel sound. These exercises help us feel the mask, so we can make sure it's resonating when we sing.

Play with Your Voice

Now that you are familiar with each of the three different vocal registers and resonators, tune in to them when you sing. Try singing different phrases in a variety of ways, engaging various parts of the body. Sometimes if I'm trying to hit a note in the upper end of my middle voice, it sounds better if I lighten up, soften the tone, and sing in a lighter head voice instead. It depends on the context, but it's important to give yourself the freedom to explore different approaches.

And as you do, tune in to your body and the shifting ways in which it's vibrating. This body-centred awareness becomes an anchor for mindfulness, giving us a visceral point of focus to bring us into the present moment. This then becomes a tool we carry in our waking lives, tuning in to our bodies repeatedly throughout the day. This mindful way of living can change everything. The more we feel into our bodies, the more aware we become of our own needs. Waking up to our present experience enriches our lives. Each time we notice these things, we develop our awareness. Which in turn creates options. So you see? Mindful singing can change your life.

Transition Points

Remember that piano, the one representing your own unique singing voice? Not only are our vocal ranges much smaller than the 88 keys offered by a standard piano, but our three vocal ranges (chest, middle and head) have transition points in between them, places where notes can feel stuck or altogether missing. Imagine that this piano, now shrunk to about a quarter of its original size, also has a key missing every so often. Some piano! But this is your voice, for better and for worse. And those missing notes are the ones that land at the transition points between our vocal registers – they are more challenging to sing clearly, especially as we transition up and down our vocal scale. To be fair, many of our vocal 'pianos' aren't really missing notes, and with practice we can learn to sing each note in our range clearly. Learning to smooth out our vocal transition points can lead to a more polished sound.

Transition points are important to understand, and as we become more familiar with our vocal range, we can begin to experiment with different ways of singing a particular note or phrase. For example, we can sing exactly the same note at the upper end of our middle voice or with the lower end of our head voice. The note will be the same, but the quality will sound different. Neither is better or worse than the other, but one may offer more power, control or expression, given the larger context in which we are singing.

As we consider which register we want to use to sing any particular note, 'zoom back' from the music, taking a broader view of this specific phrase. By considering the context in which this specific note falls, it can be helpful to remember the notes coming both before and after the transition note that is giving us trouble. The context may impact the register with which we choose to sing a particular passage.

EXERCISE

OVER THE WATERFALL

After taking a full breath, sing the highest note you can manage (men, go to your falsetto voice), then allow the note to fall over the waterfall, descending in pitch all the way to the lowest note you can sing. Try doing this with only one breath. Now do it again, noticing the points where your voice shifts from one register to another. In men, the most obvious break occurs at the low end of the falsetto range, as the larynx seems to 'jump' into the next register.

Caring for the Body

◆

Singing can be hard work for our vocal cords, and their efforts are deserving of a little nurturing. As we would before and after any other form of exercise, we should warm up, cool down and treat our bodies with care.

A QUICK ONLINE SEARCH of expensive auction items reveals rare musical instruments costing millions of pounds. Imagine owning one of those, and the lengths to which you would go to ensure its protection, keeping it in top working condition, thereby preserving (if not increasing) its overall value. If we have the financial resources to afford such an instrument, we would also likely spare no expense in keeping it safe, secure and operating in top condition.

Your voice is the most expensive instrument around

Now, I realize that many of us don't believe our voices are valued at the same level as a rare violin. And as such, many of us smoke, drink, scream and live our normal human lives without much regard for the impact it has on our vocal chords. But now that we're singing (right?), now that we trust that our voices provide a pathway to a more vibrant, present and engaged life (right?), we need to show them the same respect we would the most expensive instrument around. Maybe even more so.

Health Warning

Our voice is the only one we get, and there are some types of damage we can do through abuse, neglect and incorrect singing that cause irreparable harm. So please take notice: if your voice becomes sore and achy, dry or tender, those can be signs of vocal fatigue or injury. Similarly, if your voice becomes raspy or you can no longer hit some of the notes at either end of your vocal range, those too can be a signal that it's time to take better care of your voice, or possibly institute more vocal rest. Let's make sure we stay ahead of the vocal-care game by following these ten easy tips for caring for that most precious of musical instruments, your voice.

I know a famous singer in the United States who takes the final tip on my list to a new level, refusing to talk for hours after his performances. Now, this gentleman is a renowned talent and has one of the more powerful and unique voices around. It doesn't surprise me that he would elevate vocal care to an art form. But I will say, news of this man's practice came to me in the form of a complaint from a friend of mine. She was so excited to finally have a chance to meet him back stage after the show, only to find that he refused to utter even a single word to any one of the VIPs in attendance. But when you hear him sing, you can understand why he takes vocal care so seriously.

Our voice is the only one we get. Let's make sure we stay ahead of the vocal-care game

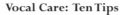

Vocal Care: Ten Tips

1. Start with gentle warm-up exercises for both the high and low ends of your vocal register. Take your time, ease into it.

2. Avoid excessive intake of alcohol, soft drinks or coffee. These substances can dry out and stress the vocal chords.

3. Smoking should be avoided for many reasons, but nicotine also increases the production of mucus, which interferes with the clear vocal tone we're aiming for.

4. Use a humidifier in your home; thirty per cent humidity is preferable. Your vocal chords will thank you.

5. Stay hydrated. This one is an important part of a healthy body and relaxed vocal chords.

6. Avoid pushing your voice. Remember that it is possible to place an undue burden on our vocal chords. Be gentle.

7. Beware of allergies to pets, dust, mould and other pollutants. They can wreak havoc on our voices.

8. Consume a healthy and balanced diet. Doing so provides the vitamins and minerals our body needs to keep our vocal chords supple and agile.

9. Enjoy a cup of hot tea after singing, which provides a soothing rub down for your vocal structures after a workout.

10. Rest. The amount of sleep we get affects the strength, tone and quality of our singing voices and learning to provide adequate rest for our voices after singing is vital.

THE BODY BALANCE

◆

Among the most tangible benefits of regular mindful singing involve the transformative impact it has on the body. Not only does singing make us feel better mentally, emotionally and physically, but it also deepens the connection we experience with our physicality.

A S ALLUDED TO EARLIER, my graduate degrees involved studying topics such as meditation, body awareness and all things related to music, human development and psychotherapy. At our graduation ceremony, one of my colleagues said, in her brief 'thank you' speech to the audience, 'I would like to thank all of those professors who reintroduced me to my body. Sadly, I had forgotten that I had one.' We all chuckled, both because of how silly it sounded to forget you had a body, but also because we all resonated with the idea of becoming somewhat detached from our bodies, our awareness often disconnected from their rhythmic and ancient wisdom. We tend to live in our heads instead, consumed with thought and memory.

Singing engages the body whether we're sitting, standing, driving in the car or lying down on our backs. It wakes us up, vibrating melodic energy into every one of our billions of cells! Singing is a major mobilizing force, galvanizing emotional, mental and physical energy, bringing us into the present moment and opening up our hearts.

When we sing, our body buzzes in healthy and enjoyable ways. And those buzzes can be magnified when we learn and practise proper singing techniques. By 'proper', I'm talking about some basics: standing erect, feet firmly planted on the ground, knees gently bent, chin slightly tucked, sternum raised (see 'The Garcia Position' on page 70), core muscles engaged for breath support – all of this involves the focused use of many parts of the body, and it can be exhausting. But if you stick with it, practising a little every day, it's worth it.

Mastering Technique

One thing I learned in my formative years as a piano player: when learning something new, it's far better to play (or sing) the song very slowly and with correct form than it is to speed it up and risk reinforcing incorrect techniques. The brain is a learning machine, and we really want it to learn the correct patterns the first time. Working retroactively to 'un-learn' certain patterns is often an uphill slog, and one to be avoided whenever possible. So let's slow down, correctly practise some of the basics of proper singing and set ourselves up for the years of joy that are to come when we have a connected, controlled singing voice.

Mindful singing is about balance. As we learn to support vocal tone with the strength and support of our core muscles, the rest of singing is about relaxation. The importance of this cannot be overstated. In addition to relaxing our throat, neck,

---

EXERCISE

THE GARCIA POSITION

Stand comfortably and with space around you. Raise your arms in front of you, high above your head. Really stretch, keeping your feet flat on the ground. Then slowly lower your arms, wrapping them behind your back, all the while trying not to move your sternum from its raised position. With your palms facing outward, place your hands one on top of the other, both resting on your tailbone (sacrum). This is called the Garcia position. This leaves your heart space open, your ribcage raised, your shoulders square, your back straight. When you first lower your arms, this posture will feel rather exaggerated, and it's likely that you'll settle into a more natural position as you sing. But this exercise will give you the proper feel. Now sing your favourite song and notice the difference.

---

shoulders and head, we're also aiming to relax the tongue when we sing. This is important for two reasons. First, holding tension in our body will alter our voice, constricting the tone a bit and shifting away from the open, full sound we want to produce. Second, an engaged tongue blocks the sound. Now, of course the tongue will be naturally engaged to some degree while singing, especially while pronouncing the lyrics. But when the tongue is anywhere but resting gently and flatly on the floor of the mouth, it's in the way, compromising the shape of the tone.

Balancing all of these new ways of singing is a lot to think about at first, I know. Stick with the basics: gently engage the core for breath support, and relax the rest of the muscles.

Uplifted

Not only can singing be uplifting in the emotional sense, but it's anatomically accurate as well. If we're singing correctly, our bodies as well as our spirits will become uplifted. In the body specifically, I'm talking about the sternum, our upper chest and our ribcage.

This expansive singing posture is also a nice reflection of the open-hearted way in which we are striving to live. Open chest, vulnerable heart, facing forward, ready to meet the world, supporting ourselves with the breath, using our voices with authenticity and integrity to speak and sing our deeper truths. This is how we sing, this is how we live: presently, mindfully, musically, gratefully.

CHAPTER THREE

HEALING SONGS

It's a fact: singing is healthy,
regardless of how we think it sounds.
Singing familiar songs we know and love connects
us to our bodies and emotions in ways that words alone
can never do. Even when we sing unfamiliar music or
improvise with sound, the vibrations themselves affect
our bodies in profound and healing ways. So let us set
aside that story we've been told that says 'we can't
sing'. Instead, let us be guided by the ancient
wisdom of our bodies towards the sacred
expression of our authentic sound.

SINGING IS GOOD FOR US

◆

When it comes to things that make us feel good, singing is one of the best. It serves us on every level, from the physical to the spiritual. Singing is sacred and it can also be silly — but whatever we call it, it benefits us when we do it regularly.

SINGING ALONG WITH FAMILIAR SONGS, singing in a group, singing alone, even singing without words leaves us feeling better than we did before. It's like taking a walk. I don't think I've ever regretted taking a walk, having always felt refreshed afterwards. Singing is like that. It doesn't seem to matter whether I sing happy songs or sad songs, original songs or covers. Singing always leaves me feeling better than I did before.

Singing is really good for us, the evidence is irrefutable. It may actually be one of those rare activities that have few, if any, adverse side-effects except for singing incorrectly and damaging the vocal chords. Or those relational challenges we associate with being vulnerable and therefore potentially embarrassing. But we won't let that stop us, right? Right?

The Scientific Stuff

Singing affects our moods, our bodies, our brains, everything. It releases endorphins and other feel-good hormones including oxytocin, which is considered to be the bonding hormone, increasing our sense of connection with others. It increases oxygen to the brain, expands our lungs and engages vital muscle groups throughout our body. And the multitude of benefits doesn't stop with us. It even affects the air and the life around us. And the majority of the research points to group singing (i.e. singing in a chorale or choir) as providing the most benefits of all. This may explain the recent increase in the numbers of people joining choirs around the world. More people singing in the world gives me hope for humanity.

Putting this all together for a moment: everything in the universe is vibrating and singing, we all respond to music in positive ways and secretly (or not) love to sing, and singing is really good for us on every level. So what's the problem? Why aren't we all walking through the world singing our own personal, awesome soundtrack? Well, some of us are, I suppose. And I tip my hat to you if you happen to be one of them. But most of us aren't singing our own soundtrack, unabashedly, in all of our full-throated majesty. In fact, many of us, if we sing at all, sing sparingly, usually alone, or we have stopped singing altogether.

Why Do We Stop Singing?

To be fair, some of us aren't singing because we tried it, didn't like it, and that, as they say, was that. Although my therapist side becomes instantly curious about *why* we didn't like it. Because our souls did, our hearts did and our bodies did, too.

The truth is that for most of us something else happened along the way. Sometimes we remember what that something was, and other times not. Often, the sensations, beliefs and stories that stop us from singing with a full voice live in us as a felt sense rather than a coherent narrative. Our wounds become implied memories, lurking in the background but colouring those things with which we are willing to engage. We don't *want* to sing. So we don't. We aren't comfortable, for whatever reason. And the idea of it makes us turn away and desperately seek a change in subject. What happened to us, and how can we shift what seems like an age-old automatic response? How can simple mindfulness practices unleash the joy that our voices are waiting to express?

EXERCISE

TONING

Toning is a singing technique where we sing without words, but with open vowel sounds to experience the vibrations throughout the body. Try toning for five straight minutes. Use both higher and lower notes, and try a variety of vowel sounds including *Oh*, *Ooh*, *Ah* and *Ae*. Notice the different parts of the body that resonate with each new vocal tone, and notice the way that your body seems to be vibrating when you've finished.

SINGING & MEDITATION

◆

My mind is like an open body of water, quickly agitated and not so easily soothed. When disturbed, all I can see is the commotion on the surface, the foaming waves. But when it settles, I can peer into its depths and know myself more fully.

SOMETIMES PEOPLE MISTAKENLY BELIEVE that meditation is solely devoted to promoting a sense of inner peace and calm. And while regular practitioners certainly experience these states more commonly than others, to focus solely upon them as the 'goal' of meditation misses the point. The larger context is that medita-tion increases our awareness of ourselves – our bodies, our thoughts, our feelings, our environment – and of others. And through the regular application of breath and awareness, our relationship with these things shifts. In fact, our relationship with all things shifts, and that, my friends, is the point. It's not that we won't be angry, we learn how to relate differently to our thoughts and feelings relative to anger.

Make space for every thought and emotion

This can become true for everything. Rather than chasing the illusion than we can exist in a perpetual state of calm, those of us on a mindful path make space for every type of thought and emotion. We breathe, and observe more than we react. This takes practice, of course, which is why we dedicate

'I Learned to Meditate'

I used to work with a young woman who, while supremely capable at her job, was often highly anxious throughout the day. She talked quickly, she moved quickly, she was highly productive but also flighty – frequently misplacing things or failing to complete her sentences before another frantic idea popped into her mind. Our paths went separate ways, but when I saw her years later, she was remarkably different. She was breathing more slowly, making more eye contact, giving a thoughtful pause before speaking. When I summoned the courage to ask her what had changed, she smiled and replied, 'I learned to meditate.'

ourselves not just to making time for daily reflection but also to bringing this mindful lens with us throughout our day. This is how we care for our minds. By keeping them in the present as much as possible.

Practising awareness allows us to observe these shifting phenomena without judgement. We are able to notice the transient nature of thoughts and feelings, caring for them and accepting them. The more we are able to practise this simple way of noticing during our day, the more fulfilling our day can become. And of all the ways we can practise meditation and awareness, singing is perhaps the most fun. In addition to the neurological benefits, we also know that singing can both calm and energize our minds. It can wake us and help us feel more present and alert, while also decreasing symptoms of anxiety and promoting feelings of relaxation, calm and well-being. This is another way we care for the mind, by singing.

Learning to Live with Grace

When I first started meditating, I was under the mistaken impression that if I were self-disciplined enough to sit quietly for twenty minutes each day, then I could tick that box and

---

EXERCISE

MINDFUL VOICE

Start this meditation by taking a few calm, slow, smooth breaths. For the next five minutes, sit silently watching your breath go in and out, your chest rising and falling. As thoughts bubble up in your mind, simply label them as 'thinking', and return to your breath. Repeatedly. After five minutes, begin to create sound with your voice. First very quietly and with a hum. Feel those vibrations, notice how far they travel in your body. Then slowly increase the volume, open the mouth, and allow yourself to sing some more – either a song you know or something improvised. It could be nonsense words or discernible lyrics. The idea is simply to drop yourself into a very mindful, present space first, then bring that awareness to your voice as you slowly add the sound.

---

get back to living my regular life. It took more time for me to understand that while those twenty daily minutes are indeed important and do make a noticeable difference in my life, the idea is for me to bring that sense of mindful awareness with me throughout my day, wherever I go. After all, what's the point in sitting quietly for twenty minutes, cultivating loving-kindness and compassion, if I then resort to yelling at that idiotic driver in front of me a mere twenty minutes later? This is why meditators *practise* their mindful approaches to living. Presence and compassion are not something to be mastered; this is an ongoing commitment to a conscious lifestyle where we learn to tune in and notice in ever more refined detail the magical nuances of each passing moment.

Meditations may take many forms, each of them designed with the purpose of waking us up, bringing our awareness more fully into the present moment, and helping us to observe our thoughts and feelings without the need to change them. Through mindful living, we are repeatedly given the opportunity to relax into acceptance of ourselves and others, and we learn to live with grace.

Learn to tune in and notice in ever more refined detail the magical nuances of each passing moment

SINGING FROM THE HEART

◆

Singing from the heart requires us to set aside our social armour, leaving us unbearably exposed. But those places that frighten us also hold our greatest treasure. Learning to sing with mindfulness and with an open heart transforms something as common as a song into something as transcendent as a prayer.

WITH INNUMERABLE WAYS FOR THE human soul to express itself, we are all drawn to someone who is courageous enough to reveal theirs with passion, clarity and the raw vulnerability that comes with being seen and understood by others on deep levels. Whether through a poem, a dance, a musical or theatrical performance, or the myriad of other ways that our beautifully unique human expression manifests, we can tell the difference between an authentic passion and something artificial. We can feel the difference instantly, and sensing another's truth awakens something

◆

Do not ask yourself what the world needs.

Ask yourself what makes you come alive and then go

and do that. Because what the world needs is

people who have come alive.

HOWARD THURMAN (1899–1981)
AFRICAN AMERICAN AUTHOR, PHILOSOPHER AND CIVIL RIGHTS LEADER

◆

EXERCISE

VOCAL STRINGS

This is a wordless sing-along, and your voice is going to be a vowel-singing instrument. Choose a piece of familiar music, and play it either through speakers or headphones. While listening with your eyes closed, allow yourself a few seconds simply to listen. Allow the song to engage your body with its familiar rhythm and resonant chords. When you're ready, keep your eyes closed and sing along using vowel sounds such as *Ah*, *Oh* or *Ooh*. Pretend you are a string instrument, not a singing voice. You can use your instrument to play the melody line of the vocals (if the music has vocals), follow other harmony lines or make up your own. The idea is to sing from the heart and body, less from the thinking mind that engages when we sing lyrics. Try this exercise with different types of music.

---

within us. We stop and pay attention, even if for a moment, and are reminded of our own magnificence, perhaps lying dormant and unexpressed.

We don't always think of it this way, of course. Sometimes, instead of reflecting about our own gifts, we feel like we stop and stare in awe because, well, 'I can't do that. But look at them! Wow!'

Witnessing another human being 'going for it' with all they have awakens our own dreams and unexpressed desires. Some of us both admire and resent the achiever, especially if we ourselves have become disconnected from following our own passions. If we are living with a sense of regret for not chasing our own dreams, we're more tempted to tear others down. Instead, let us be inspired by everyone and everything that wakes us up, tunes us in and makes us feel alive.

The Greatest Gift

We'll revisit the power of singing with an open heart in the next chapter, but I contend that singing with an open heart is one of the greatest gifts we can give to ourselves and others. Singing is an open-hearted activity, requiring vulnerability no matter how it is done. Yet the more mindful and connected with ourselves we become, the more our songs reflect this impassioned spirit of our being. Sing your heart out each and every time. I write this simply, as if it's easy to do.

But it's not, we all know that. If singing is scary for us, then singing with a mindful, open heart is even more frightening. Some of this has to do with our inner critic, where we become mired in our own judgemental thoughts about how our voices sound. When we entertain self-critical thoughts, our bodies become constricted, which is the opposite of what we're striving for.

A Creative Outlet

As a songwriter, I put a lot of my energy into the crafting of the lyrics, wanting all of the words and phrases to impact in creative and rhythmic ways, in addition to conveying the

The Things that Matter

It has become cliché to talk about those things that matter most in life – people, experiences, connections – yet the magic of falling in love with another person, for example, is that it simultaneously tunes us in to our own hearts, reminding us that we are, at our core, love personified. Singing provides another beautiful reminder that we are here, that we matter and that our connections to others matter even more.

meaning I'm trying to express. But even if you aren't writing and performing your own songs, singing is still a powerful vehicle for the expression of emotions.

Part of the magic of music is that it has an ingenious way of sneaking past our typical defence mechanisms. Sound and rhythm find their way in, even if we didn't mean to let that happen. As singers, what we convey with our vocal tones says much more about our authentic inner workings than anything to do with words. Admittedly, this is why many of us have allowed our voices to grow quiet, fearing the repercussions that come along with being seen in our vulnerability.

But as we summon our courage, as we allow our voices to become more present in our lives, we find that our emotional world reaps the benefits. Singing makes us feel good, in part because of the chemical reactions that happen when we sing.

But singing also provides us with a creative outlet for self-expression — our song is us, it's what *we* sound like. Our singing voices are sacred; they awaken our spirits, move our emotions, engage our minds and connect us with everything else in the universe.

THE MUSIC YOU'RE MAKING

◆

The unavoidable heartache that inevitably comes with being human encourages many of us to assume protective postures, covering our hearts, quietening our voices. We get hurt, then we retreat and grow quiet. There are many ways to counteract this natural tendency and singing is the most rewarding.

B Y VIRTUE OF EVERYTHING WE KNOW up to this point about relationships and their vibrational nature, you can't help but see, hear and *feel* the music someone is making. Even when they aren't saying a word. If you want to know how someone is feeling inside, pay close attention to what it *feels* like to be around them. Remember that co-worker I mentioned earlier, the one who was productive yet exceedingly anxious? I felt myself grow nervous and constricted each time she entered the room. Similarly, when someone is critical of others, it's simply the outward manifestation of their internal landscape.

Feel the music someone is making

As we begin to understand this as adults, it provides a human context to our hurtful experiences, potentially removing some of the sting. But the pain is still there when we feel affronted, and we tend to hold on to it, subconsciously enjoying the self-righteousness that comes with feeling wronged.

How It Works

Part of this has to do with our basic psychological make-up. Certain 'reward centres' of the brain are stimulated when we blame others and when we create a narrative to explain our experiences. In our need to make sense of the world, we tell ourselves stories to understand what happened, providing a context to our emotional experiences in any given moment. When we do so, we are often rewarded with pleasurable chemicals in the brain, even when our narrative is centred upon blaming others. This can become a slippery slope of sorts, as we run the risk of becoming chemically addicted to certain psychological or emotional states that don't generally serve us. Even identifying ourselves as a victim can become an object of attachment like anything else. Victimhood can become our identity. And many of us, even when we develop the awareness that we have some of these tendencies, find that we are resistant to letting them go.

So how can we avoid being consumed by our victimhood? The solution is simple. Instead of remaining in the story that we're telling ourselves about being wronged, we return to the present moment, to our bodies, to our voices, repeatedly. We sing, and we tune in to the inherent vulnerability that comes with it. How we think and feel about ourselves shows up in our songs. Mindful singing makes it harder to hide.

As singers, it is vital that we do our own internal personal work – constantly striving to better understand ourselves, our hearts and our voices. For only by turning again and again towards our deeper selves, gently tending to our relational wounds, can we unleash the fully resonant and amazing power that comes with our voices.

GESTALT

◆

Mindful singing requires us to manage simultaneous relationships with our bodies, our voices, the song and potentially also with other people. These relationships matter, in part because we need each other on every level, and the science behind that truth is irrefutable: our systems are hardwired for relationship.

IN THE SUMMER OF 2000 I moved from Seattle to Boulder, Colorado, for many reasons, but the most obvious inspiration was to attend graduate school at Naropa University. I was, of course, enthralled with the surrounding mountains, canyons and very fishable streams, and as a fly fisherman, I dreamed of all the many ways a life in Boulder would enhance my experiential education in the years to come.

As a graduate student in the music therapy department, there were some classes I didn't have chance to take. One of them had an odd German-sounding name and I remember my friend emerging from that class a bit bleary-eyed, worn out, but half-smiling. 'What's going on?' I asked. 'Gestalt,' he said with a nod, as if that settled the matter. He passed me by, leaving me more confused than before I had asked the question.

Fast-forward three months: I am a student in the two-year training programme in Gestalt Therapy. I was correct when I said it sounded German. Gestalt Therapy is an experiential form of therapy developed by German psychotherapist Fritz Perls, among others. It builds upon the work of Martin Buber and his exploration of the *I-Thou Relationship,* a relationship between the self and the other. Using the present-moment

---

EXERCISE

THE GRATEFUL SONG

Before singing, take a few moments, allow yourself to relax and your heart to fall open. Think of someone you love dearly, perhaps even someone who has passed on, and allow your heart to open with the grateful thought of thank you, thank you, thank you. Enjoy the spaciousness that accompanies gratitude for a moment before you sing. Let this open-hearted energy influence your tone. Keep returning to the simple words, thank you.

I Am Challenged

I am seated in the centre of the room as the 'client', facing another student who is my 'therapist' for this 'working' we are doing. Around the edges of the room sit two of my trainers – veteran therapists who are teaching at the Gestalt Institute – and ten of my peers, all bearing witness to the experience I'm having in front of them. Some of them are taking notes, because we're all students-in-training and we're learning through observation as well as experience. Being in the middle of the fishbowl is always rather intimidating, but this group is familiar and vulnerability is the norm here. Everyone has their shoes off, we're all seated comfortably on pillows and cushions, and I'm in the middle of my working.

'Sing it instead,' says my therapist. I pause. 'What?' I scoff, as if his suggestion is absurd, and I feel myself blushing as I squirm and stall for time. Some part of my mind is suddenly taking an inventory of the people in the room, specifically wondering whether there are any musicians seated around me. You know, the kind who might judge me the way I judge myself, or so my mind tells me. I'm also mentally scanning the room for my anchors – those with whom I connect most deeply and before whom I bare my soul more readily. For that's what singing is, at least for me. The baring of my soul. I feel self-conscious every time I do it. And I may love to sing, but I don't do it easily. I realize too, as I'm scanning the room, that I'm also stalling for time.

My therapist repeats himself more forcefully, and this time adds almost tauntingly, 'You're a singer, right?' And I freeze. I don't want to sing. I can't sing. Not in front of people!

experience between therapist and client, Gestalt seeks to help the client become more aware about how he or she responds, moment-by-moment, in relationship.

Old Wounds

On the one hand, insecurity was an odd thing for me to be feeling during this process. Because at the time, I had sung in front of people hundreds of times in choirs, musicals, jazz groups, bluegrass bands and also as a solo singer-songwriter. Much of the time, I was comfortable with my voice, and using it in front of others. But in this moment, I wasn't really my twenty-six-year-old graduate-student self. I had flashed back to being my fourteen-year-old self, working my summer job, listening to headphones and singing along. I took them off when I saw my co-workers laughing and looking at me. 'What's so funny?' I said, as I stopped the music. But something in me already knew and I braced for it. They laughed again and muttered, 'You can't sing, man. You're terrible!' Ouch. I froze, feeling insufferably exposed, humiliated and enraged. I didn't know whether to say something spiteful, laugh it off or run away and never sing again.

Lose your mind and come to your senses.

FRITZ PERLS (1893–1970)
GERMAN PSYCHIATRIST AND PSYCHOTHERAPIST

In the end, I didn't let their idiocy stop me from finding my voice. But some wounded, scared part of me did sometimes wonder if they were right in their assessment. Their comments, and the weight I gave them, shifted my relationship with my voice for a time. I became more self-critical. And for a while, I tried harder to sound like other famous singers and less like myself.

Why did I care so much about what two other kids thought about my singing voice? For two reasons, mainly. First, I was a sensitive and insecure 14-year-old boy who loved to sing. And second, because for all of us, relationships matter. Despite the value we place on our own independence, the truth is that we can't make it alone, and none of us do.

My Song, Our Song

One of the greatest blessings and mysteries about music is how it can feel so intensely personal, yet simultaneously universal in its scope. It's like love, in audible form. We feel we own that particular song, and indeed we do. It's ours, and our love is unshakeable.

OUR RELATIONSHIP WITH THE SONG is ours and ours alone, it seems, imbued with our own unique memories, feelings and associations that bind us for life. But it doesn't stop there, does it? That song doesn't only belong to me. It is also something greater, because as soon as I share it with someone else, it has the potential to become 'our song'.

And just like love, the joy of music multiplies exponentially when shared. Remember that night we attended the concert where the band played 'our song' and we shared it with thousands, all of us united through melody, poetry and our beautifully present voices? Music brings us together, dropping us into our hearts and allowing us to feel and express certain truths that live well beyond words. When we respond with our own unique voices, the uplifted experience can become truly transcendent. Music, more than any other art form, provides a direct opportunity for connection with ourselves, with those around us and with the Divine. One phenomenon underlying this fact is called the 'Iso Principle'.

The Iso Principle

Often used by a music therapist working with a client, the Iso Principle is a concept in which the therapist improvises music in the moment to mirror the ever-changing state of their client. This could mean their physical state, in which music is matched to the client's physical movements. Or the music can also be used to reflect an underlying emotional state, like using minor chords to mirror sadness. The effect is that the music itself creates the connection and becomes the wordless bridge between two people. This bridging effect is one of the many magical properties of music – it has a natural ability to sneak past our typical defences, reaching out to us even if we're feeling defensive and obstinate. We hear the tones and feel the vibrations and our bodies respond automatically. We can't help it, and we're not supposed to help it. We are, after all, made of music.

Even in those instances when we're feeling stubborn, we can hardly help but tap our toe when an infectious rhythm starts up. It engages us. We can't not hear it. If someone starts singing our favourite song but cuts off in the middle of the chorus, our brains will take over and fill in the blank. Even if for some reason we're cross and 'not talking to' that person. Our toes will tap, our brains will hear the melody. It's not conscious, we can't help it. We are musical beings created of pulse, tone and rhythm, who love to dance and sing. And the Iso Principle provides a beautiful pathway for connection, even when met with initial resistance.

The following story provides a concrete illustration of what each of us already knows to be true: music works. We can't help but listen, and when we find the genre and tempo of music that really fits our style, many things become possible. It pulls our heads and our hearts into relationship whether we 'want to' or not. And from these spaces of connection, the music has the power to move us in many different directions. Some of us may even grow so bold as to entertain the notion of singing in public. And that's a different beast altogether, presenting its own challenges, wonders and vulnerabilities. But if we persevere, we also find that using our singing voices with others is where the real magic of singing lives.

Connecting with Danny

As I emerge from my office and step into my waiting room, I am greeted by the mother of my seven-year-old client, Danny. This little boy has moderate autism and his mother has brought him to me for a music therapy session. We are working towards goals related to emotional regulation, a reduction in temper tantrums and an increase in his verbalizations. But before any of that, I have to connect with Danny, who is currently hiding under one of the chairs in my waiting room, refusing to come into my office.

Normally I have two options at my disposal: my voice and my body. I could use my voice to ask him to come in to my office or demand he 'stop hiding this instant!' Or I could pull him from his hiding spot against his wishes. While I have a good working relationship with both Danny and his mother, I'm thankful for the third tool I have: music. Danny and I both love music.

I crouch down on the ground to make eye contact, but he sees me and turns away. I try singing my greeting to Danny (which has worked in the past), but no luck. Danny won't budge.

I take a deep breath, and listen to my intuition. I'm aware of his mother's eyes; simultaneously saying 'Now you see what I deal with every day?' and 'Please help. You're the professional here!'

Music. Danny loves music. And I happen to have my guitar with me today. After retrieving it, I sit on the floor beside Danny and watch him closely. He's not giving me much. Still turned towards the wall, barely moving, intractable. But even when we're trying not to move or give anything away, we can't help it. We're still in constant motion. Our hearts are still pumping, our lungs still breathing. And that's the type of motion that I can use.

I begin to gently pluck some notes on my guitar, matching my rhythm to Danny's breathing. He may not be aware of what I'm doing, but it doesn't matter. Danny is like all of us – helpless against the power of music. We hear a beat we like and we can't help but move along with it. It gets in our bones and we become connected with the song, and through the song, with each other.

I continue to play, watching Danny's body very closely and matching my picking to any movement or action he gives me. Soon Danny starts to move. He shifts his body, balls up a fist and hits the floor in what appears to be frustration. I see his movement coming, however, and I time the music with the movement, punctuating his fist on the floor with a loud and sharp knock on the guitar. Then I fall silent for a moment. Danny gets what just happened and he laughs. He hits the ground again and I match him with the guitar. Then again, and again and with more laughter. Soon he turns to make eye contact with me and we both smile. In the next moment, he's emerging from his hiding spot and walking with me into my office. And with each step he takes, I strum the guitar, providing the soundtrack to his movements, which have more than a little happiness in them.

CHAPTER FOUR

THE COURAGE TO BE HEARD

*Vulnerability assumes many forms. Saying
I love you. Saying I'm sorry. Sharing from the heart.
Standing naked before another. Allowing our singing
voices to be heard. In sharing our words, we feel
understood. Being witnessed in our birthday suit makes
us feel seen. And in sharing our voices, the most sacred
of instruments, we have the potential to feel heard,
seen, understood and connected in ways that go well
beyond words and bodies. Our voices carry our deepest
truths, which is why it is both intimidating and
necessary that we allow them to be heard.*

IT'S ALL IN YOUR MIND

◆

There are few things I enjoy more in life than live music. Whether it's a solo artist singing in a coffee shop, street performers playing for pennies or a stadium band sharing their music with the masses, live music is the one thing that makes me stop and pay attention.

WITH SO MANY DIFFERENT WAYS of being human and the unending possibilities of combining musical tones, the opportunities for creative musical expression are endless. Yet each of us has heard a very small snippet of music, something we've never heard before but are instantly drawn to. We want to hear more. Every universal human experience, those deep feelings that all of us have but few of us can fully articulate, are alive in the music, plucking the strings of our own hearts. We hear that sound and something within us says, *I know that feeling. I have also felt like that.* And we are drawn in, connected, effortlessly. These unconscious connections to the musician and composer occur in sound, and they bind us in ways that defy reason.

We can have these experiences of feeling profoundly moved by music when listening to a recording as well as when experiencing a live performance. They each have their own benefits. But the live performance is so different, and the human connection that happens through sound is both palpable and ineffable, just like love.

If I cannot fly, let me sing.

FROM 'SWEENEY TODD: THE DEMON BARBER OF FLEET STREET'
STEPHEN SONDHEIM

The Best of Times, the Worst of Times

In the best of times, singing can make us feel euphoric. Whether you're the one on stage, or the one in the audience, falling into a shared groove and experiencing life through songs is powerful magic. It opens our hearts, connects us with our voices and stimulates our senses, bringing us much more fully into the joyful present moment. But that's in the best of times.

In the worst of times, singing leaves us feeling fearfully intimidated, even suddenly mute in the face of the crushing vulnerability that often accompanies a live performance. The very thought of singing in public is enough to make many people squirm. I have performed hundreds of times and whether I am singing before an audience of one or several thousand, it's always scary to sing.

Waking the Inner Critic

Sharing our voices takes tremendous courage, and it is certain to awaken our inner critic — that inner voice that tears us down, harps on our mistakes, insisting that we shouldn't sing because we're not good enough. The inner critic is sneaky and

Finding Courage

As a child who loved to sing, I used to imagine singing the National Anthem at a professional sporting event, visualizing what it would be like to have all of those pairs of eyes locked on to me. Intimidating? Certainly. Exhilarating? Absolutely! Years later that dream became a reality, and I learned that allowing our voices to be heard by thousands or by one is the same terrifying endeavour, requiring the same courage.

---

insatiable, always on the lookout for a missed note or a botched lyric; any invitation to remind us we're not perfect. *Aha! You screwed up and people heard it! They know you make mistakes!* These are the same fears that stop some kids from ever raising their hand in the classroom. *What if my answer is wrong? What if people laugh? I'll be humiliated! Best to not even try. I'll just become silent, invisible. That's safer.*

But when that becomes the pattern, when we shut ourselves down in the face of vulnerability, we become disconnected. And we know where that pathway tends to lead – sadness, despair, isolation, depression, addiction. We need people, that's all there is to it. We require connection to thrive. The challenging part is that creating deep connection also requires openness, truth, trust and vulnerability. Just like sharing our voices, and singing in public.

Stage Fright

Singing in front of others is a lot like being naked. In fact, when I'm sharing my original songs in front of an audience, the vulnerability is so palpable that at times it would be easier to stand up there in my birthday suit, rather than opening my heart, unleashing my voice and sharing my soul. But by learning to swim in these vulnerable waters, we can enter into the magical realms of deep intimacy and profound connection.

Before that's possible, however, we have to learn to deal with the fear and anxiety that comes with stage fright. Everybody gets nervous about sharing their voices, but turning to mindfulness practices reminds our bodies to stay relaxed and open. Without these practices, the body does what is natural in the face of fear and anxiety: it holds tension and prepares us for action. We can compensate for this with regular practice of mindfulness exercises.

EXERCISE

SINGING THROUGH TENSION

Take a moment to notice your breath as it is right now. Don't change how you're breathing, just become aware. Now conjure up a time you felt critical of another and bring up that resentful feeling. Notice where it lives in your body. Pay attention to that place as you begin to sing, and notice what happens to it as you continue.

Even Tempo

There are certainly performances where no matter how many mindfulness practices I do, I cannot completely settle my nerves before walking out on stage. To be honest, this happens regularly. At that point, I keep breathing, and as I'm working my way through the first song, I remind myself to slow down. Nervous energy tends to speed things along and I want to fight against that unconscious impulse. Instead, I may even feel like I'm playing the song a little too slowly. But in these conditions, I'll settle for too slowly, as it gives me a chance to relax into the groove, into the energy of being on stage in front of people, and into my body. I can genuinely trust that if I keep breathing, keep feeling my body, keep working my way through the song, my nerves will settle before long. This sometimes happens by the end of the first song and rarely later than the end of the second.

Singing in public can be a phenomenal experience, for you as well as the audience, and the more we do it, the more enjoyable it can become. The sharing of our voices, the interactions with the audiences, these dynamic experiences get at the heart of what it means to be human, and summoning the courage to be creative and vulnerable in front of others always pays dividends.

My dear friend is a very talented artist who is making a successful living by selling his creations — those he makes in his home studio, in his own time, at his own speed, with his own vision. Yet when asked directly by someone if he is 'an artist', he often demurs, responding instead, 'Well, I make art.' There's something funny that happens for each of us around owning our identities. 'Well, I sing' feels safer than 'I am a singer'. But seeing as how we are dedicated to mindfulness and courage, try it: I am a singer. Breathe. Then sing.

IT'S ALL IN THE EAR

Most people, when asked if they are able to sing, will reply with something other than 'yes' or 'absolutely!' Perhaps you're one of them. Many downplay it, respond with a 'not really' or 'not very well' or 'only in the shower' — and others respond with something more akin to 'No freaking way!'

SADLY, SINGING HAS BECOME THIS THING that we think only the professionals should do, leaving the rest of us to cower in our muted shame because we're not good enough. We're not worthy. No one wants to listen to us sing. So we turn it down. Or worse, we turn it off. But even if you're one of those who steadfastly believes that you cannot sing no matter how hard you try, despair no longer. There's hope. And it lives in your ear.

A recent study found that only very few members of the population are actually 'tone deaf'. Which means that nearly every one of us is, in fact, capable of carrying a tune. That is,

Dependable Singers

There are some groups of people you can always count on to sing along with you. As I was going through my graduate training I lead a number of music therapy groups. Along the way, I found that the young and the old are two groups of people who always love to sing. Play a song they know, and they're guaranteed to sing along with you and move their bodies to the beat, engaged on every level. They don't care what they sound like. They love the song and allow themselves to be consumed by the music and the joy that comes with it.

Children and grandparents – the perfect audience. But what happened in between? How come so many of us have grown shy about our singing voices? Ah yes, I remember. School happened. Many years of school. And teachers. And grades. And kids who let unabashed opinions be known.

That truth, and the palpable silence brought on by bullying, is more apparent today than ever, thanks to the advent of social media. No wonder so many of us are afraid to put ourselves out there, letting our voices be heard.

Let us instead hold the vision of these dependable singers, the young and the old, and remember what it was like to embody that type of freedom. One look at their joyful faces encourages us all to say: 'Who cares what I sound like? I'm enjoying myself!' May we, too, become dependable singers.

hearing the pitch and singing that same pitch. Nearly anyone can sing a song when it's played in their range, and those of us who struggle with keeping our voices on pitch often have more of an issue with our hearing than we do with our voices.

Digital Aid

Ear training is something we can all benefit from, and there are two basic components involved: learning to *hear* the pitch you wish to sing, and then being able to control your voice well enough to match it. A digital guitar tuner is a relatively inexpensive way to practise your ear training, because it will not only play the desired note, it will also give you digital feedback on how closely matched your voice is with the 'correct' pitch. For example, it will play an A note, then as you sing the same note back, you can watch the variations in the meter based on how far away your voice is from the original target note. Using this method, beginners are often able to make noticeable progress in a relatively short time.

So we all have it in us to sing, especially when we work with our ear. If we believed we sang well, we would sing all the time without hesitation. But most of us feel less than fully confident in our singing voices. We can trace this reluctance back to several sources, all of which prey upon our inherent insecurities. Some of them are creations of our own minds, others are influences from external sources such as mass media and our recent fascination with singing competitions.

Un-reality Television

We all love talent on display, and I'll stand in line to see a gifted singer. For that reason alone, I can understand our recent obsession with 'reality television' and, in particular, singing competitions. We're always on the lookout for the best. But making a competition out of a sacred personal expression means that in order to crown the 'best', we also have to decide upon those who are the 'worst'.

And we secretly love to watch that part, don't we? The awful voices, in particular those who sing every note with confidence even though none of them are in tune? Then we watch how the judges handle the feedback and we feel a little better about our own voices. Even though we don't, really. We are judged in the same way as the contestant, either by others or by ourselves. We're always our own toughest critic. And it's easy to let the criticism get in the way of singing. It's easier to decide we just don't like to sing.

Reality television has shaped the way many of us think about talent, especially when it comes to singing. Opinions tend to converge at the extremes – the most talented among us and the least talented among us. We can all agree, for example, that Adele can sing with the best of them. You may not love her vocal style or appreciate her songs (I happen to be fond of both), but from a vocal standpoint, she can clearly sing. But sing compared to what? Well, compared to others, of course. All those who have come before, famous and not.

Comparison is a tricky business, for we can always find those who appear lesser or greater than us in any single dimension. But doing so only furthers the notion that there's something wrong with us – in this case, that we can't really sing. Until we see someone who makes us feel like we can sing with the best of them.

Why Do We Do It?

We watch singing competitions on television for a number of reasons, not the least of which is that there is something inherently inspiring about watching someone chasing their dreams, especially if it's a dream that we all secretly harbour. But we also watch for the same reason we slow our cars down to scrutinize the collision on the side of the road.

In part, we watch for the train wrecks, those unabashedly terrible performances that lead to scorn, humiliation and ridicule from the judges and audience alike. In both instances – the actual car crash and the emotional one that happens in front of the television cameras – we have the same response: we watch with rapt attention, in stupefied awe over what we're seeing, and we have two simultaneous thoughts – 'Oh my goodness, I can't believe what I'm seeing!' And, 'I'm so glad that this isn't happening to me.'

With our voices, some scared part of us goes further into thinking, 'That will never be me. I will never open myself up to scathing criticism of my singing voice. Best not to sing.

Which is fine. I'm not very good anyway.' Or so we like to believe. Because believing this lets us off the hook. We don't ever have to try, because we 'can't'.

While I am as guilty as others at having become fascinated by certain television singing competitions, I lament the impact they are having on our attitudes towards our voices. We compare ourselves with others constantly, making judgements about what's good and what's bad. And we have mistakenly come to believe that we should only expose that which is best within us – that which is polished, ready for the lights and the cameras, and ready to withstand the withering scrutiny that comes with a public unveiling.

The Place that Remembers

Comparing ourselves with others is the fastest route to unhappiness, and it's a battle we all seem destined to wage. Our brains are driven to compare, contrast and label what we're seeing and experiencing. The truth is that we can *always* find someone else who we think is better or worse than us by any particular metric. So let's stop comparing. Remember your voice is yours and yours alone. Return to your breath, come back to your senses, connect with your voice.

Let's get back to that time before school started, when we were four and five years old, when we loved to sing, draw and make believe. Before we began evaluating how *well* we could sing, draw and make believe. Give yourself permission.

Mindful Tune-up

Try singing every day for at least ten minutes, paying particular attention to how you feel before and after you sing. Be gentle with your voice, taking time to warm up and cool down.

There is still a place within you that remembers everything you need to know. This place has never forgotten how much you like to sing, and perhaps dance, draw, colour, write, sew, sculpt, play, paint, laugh, love and more. This place is creative, dynamic, and is deeply connected with everything else in the universe that is singing along. This is where your voice begins, where your songs come from, and it's a place you can learn to return to whenever you wish. It is there for you always, one simple, mindful breath away.

The Garden of Your Mind

When it comes to our gardens, if we don't purposefully plant the things we would like to grow, we end up with nothing but weeds. This is where the power of intention comes along, followed up of course by plenty of hard work. Envisioning your garden, laying out the design in your mind, making yourself a list of seeds and tools to buy, that's the intention. It helps if you focus on the details and become clear on exactly what you would like to create. This is as true for setting any goal as

it is for gardening. Clarity is crucial. Plant what you'd like to grow and nuture it with the right tools. Or prepare for the weeds to take over.

When it comes to singing, the same applies – we need to pay as much attention to our mental contents as we do to our voices if we don't want our our inner critic to claim our minds as weeds claim our gardens. Our minds are just as important as our voices and both require proper care. This is especially true if you happen to be anyone other than those lucky few who are in love with their singing voices. For the rest of us, the inner critic is likely to rear its ugly head at times. But we'll be ready and waiting when it arrives, ready to drown it out with our magnificent voices.

EXERCISE

THE SNAPSHOT TECHNIQUE

The next time your inner critic starts speaking to you, simply snap a picture in your mind – catching him or her in the act. Perhaps your inner critic has a specific form – like a specific person tied to past criticisms. Or perhaps your inner critic is more of a nebulous feeling, less specific in form but equally destructive in purpose. Either way, catching him or her in the act, like a Gotcha! moment, is the same as noticing your thoughts during a meditation. With practice, we disarm the critic of its power and return to our present selves.

How to Sing in Public

Singing at home is one thing. Singing in front of even one other human being is another thing entirely, requiring an additional skill set. Nerves, stage fright, imperfection and insecurity, it's all part of the deal. But so are infectious joy and exhilaration! Here are a few tips to help ensure you relish, rather than dread, the experience.

• Breathe. Frequently, mindfully. Before, during and after songs and in between banter with the audience. Everything flows from our awareness of the breath.

• Remember your tempo. It's easy to speed up when playing live due to the adrenaline coursing through your system.

• Drink water or hot tea on stage. Your vocal cords are not on friendly terms with caffeine, alcohol or carbonation.

• Smile. If you're having fun, make sure you tell your face.

• Open your eyes. It can be very tempting to close our eyes and feel into the song. But too much of it, and our connection with the audience suffers. I have seen performers who close their eyes throughout entire songs. And others hardly ever. Making eye contact in the middle of a song can be riveting.

• Remember your singing posture. Gently lift your ribcage, open your heart. Don't lock your knees, keep them slightly bent. Stay open and resonant.

• Above all, have fun. Go for it. Sing your heart out.

Performing with Others

◆

It's the sheer power of so many voices, singing all at the same time. Or maybe it's the interplay of harmonies, weaving in and out with dynamic precision. Perhaps it's vibration of goodwill, the natural outcome of people working together, expressing themselves, being beautiful in their vulnerability — sharing their sacred instrument.

MY SPIRITS SOARED RECENTLY when I read that, around the globe, group singing is rising in popularity. More of us singing means that not only are more people connecting with themselves and their voices, but more are also willing to share their voices publicly and use them to connect with others. This may seem like small potatoes, but to someone like me who understands and relishes in the benefits of regular singing, this is major news, the kind of news that makes me feel even more optimistic about the future of life on our planet. More people singing, more people connected, more people feeling good about themselves, others and life; this is good news for all of us. Those types of movements create benevolent ripples in the cosmic atmosphere, serving every last one of us.

If you've never had the experience, consider joining a choir or singing group in your area. The internet has made meet-up groups of any stripe available to us with little effort, and there's likely a singing group near you, even one for first-timers.

Group Singing

In group singing, the song is split up into parts, lowest to highest, with the men broken into the basses and baritones, and the women into the altos and sopranos. This is only one configuration and they don't need to be gender-specific. But you get a sense of how a song might be approached.

The magic of singing in a group is in the balance between the individual and the whole. You are one voice, singing in a smaller group of voices (say, the altos), which are part of a larger group of voices. All of us together, each contributing our own sacred instrument, to something larger and more beautiful than we could have made on our own. Just like life.

Group singing can be challenging at times, especially at first or for someone who has never tried to read music. Just like anything else, it's a learnable skill. And most people can learn to sight-read well enough to become adequate in a short amount of time. But at first, there's a lot to keep track of: there's usually a pianist playing the song, a conductor leading the group, the music you're holding in your hands, your own posture and voice, and the voices of those around you. It sounds daunting, but it's easier than you think. And much more rewarding. After the first rehearsal or two, once you make connections within the group and begin to connect through the song, the general sense of well-being that comes with it is undoubtedly worth the effort. Try it out, join a choir, sing in church, start a band, take the risk. It can change your life.

Listen!

As with ear training and singing, the success of singing with others lies in everyone's willingness to listen. This is critical for small groups like duos, trios and small bands. But even if you're singing in a large choir, listening to the other voices is an important skill to practise. Some people come by this naturally, while others may be so focused on their own voices that they can forget how to listen. Regardless of our natural tendencies, we can all benefit from more listening. The more we listen, the more we hear, and hearing allows us to play with the dynamics of a song, enhancing the production of the music with subtle shifts in volume and tone.

Our voices are sacred, using them to sing is necessary

Listening is another key component to mindful singing. We listen to our own voices, to our bodies, to the other voices, or instruments, to the room and so on. We tune in to the fact that we are the instruments, pulsating sound and rhythm, connected, dynamic and creative in this present moment. Our voices are sacred, using them to sing is necessary. Bringing mindfulness to singing is transformative and singing in a group is one of the best things you'll ever do. Put yourself out there. You won't regret it.

Consider finding even one singing or music partner in your area. Make weekly time to share music, listen to music and create music. If you're making music and want to try singing in public, explore 'open mic' events at local coffee shops and pubs. These are evenings when anyone can sign up for a few minutes of stage time, and some people read poetry or tell jokes and many share songs. It's a wonderful opportunity before a very understanding audience, and the perfect place to practise stage presence, learn about sound equipment and share your voice.

PERFORMING ON STAGE

Remember your mindfulness tools. Breathe. Drop into your body. Notice what's happening both within you and around you. Breathe again. Be here now. It's so easy to do, at least for a moment, and yet it's also so easy to forget to do, especially when you need it the most. You are on stage, live.

FEELING NERVOUS AND EXCITED, alive with anticipation, is part of the live experience, like being on a first date. Of course you're going to feel a little awkward at first, but if we remember some of our exercises, and if we bring our mindful practices to bear in moments like these, the experience can become unforgettable.

One of the more common suggestions to deal with stage fright involves simply taking a *deep* breath, which certainly can help. I have also found usefulness in both the square breath and a nice, long exhalation. Close the lips a bit, restricting the

airflow, which will in turn lengthen the time it takes to blow out all the air. And that's the point, it slows us down. How we are breathing and how we are doing in any one moment are inextricably linked. Notice our bodies, tune in to the sensations in our physical being, rather than getting caught up in the thoughts and the story we're telling ourselves about the experience we're having.

Feeling self-conscious before and during a performance is a natural part of the process, and rather than preparing as if these emotional experiences can be avoided, let's learn to ride the waves when they do make an appearance. Nerves and anxiety are fairly constant companions to performers, artists and – well, OK, humans. For it is out of our deepest vulnerabilities that shines our brightest light.

Being the singers and the courageous warriors that we are, we are willing to risk failure, or at least embarrassment. Because as we all know with live performances, anything can, and frequently does, happen. But we'll be ready. We have our tools at hand and we know how to use them, mindful singers that we are.

The Debut Performance

In my first performance (see page 118) I tightened up and lost myself, concerned more about the other people in the room than the song and the lyrics I was about to sing. I forgot about myself and my body, getting lost in my head. As I recall it, I

Going Solo

I am waiting in the wings of an exclusive music venue in Seattle. Guitar in hand, I am prepared to take to the stage for my solo performance, sharing my songs with several hundred people in attendance, including friends and family. My heartbeat quickens, my chest grows tight, and I make a conscious effort to slow my breathing. I remind myself that this feeling is excitement. The lights go down, and as I walk on stage and into the bright lights, I feel a surge of energy in my body. Yet the closer I get to the solitary microphone, the more constricted my throat becomes. I breathe.

---

made some light-hearted joke about missing the words, dived back in as quickly as I could and made it through the rest of the song without incident. But that phenomenon – losing myself in the middle of the song, letting the anxiety take over and become a distraction – is one that I continue to fight with vigilance during each and every performance.

Singing in the shower is one thing, singing in front of others is another thing entirely. Singing in front of one particular person can be very different from singing in front of another

Feeling self-conscious before and during a performance is a natural part of the process

single person. Depending upon our relationship with those in the audience, we can become more or less activated and therefore trapped in our heightened states of psychological arousal – nerves. This can feel like anxiety, nervousness, tightness, and is often accompanied by a quickening of the heartbeat as well as the racing of our thoughts, self-criticism and doubt. When all of this is happening not just before we go on stage but *while* we are performing on stage, it presents a unique set of challenges.

Expectant Faces

I am seventeen years old, and I'm sitting on a stool in the middle of a crowded coffee shop popular with students from the nearby university. My friend, another high-school student, is next to me, strumming the instrumental intro to the song we've been practising, a cover by James Taylor. I've been in a number of singing groups before, but this is my first time as a duo and I'm the only singer. My heart is pounding, the patrons are listening, and I'm trying to pay more attention to the chords my friend is playing than to the many faces surrounding me, each of them looking expectant, waiting for me to do something. The intro is over, it's time to sing. I take a breath, but my mind goes blank and no words come out. But the song keeps playing, awkwardly and without lyrics.

EXERCISE

YOU ARE ENOUGH

Think of one of your favourite singers of all time, someone you think possesses vocal abilities far beyond your own. Imagine him or her standing next to you. You're about to sing and they're about to listen. Take a breath, notice your body. Try singing part of a song for them, maintaining the visualization. The second time, visualize someone else, someone you love and who loves you. Someone who opens your heart. Feel into your heart space now as you see them clearly in your mind. When you're ready, begin to sing. Notice the difference. When we put others on a pedestal, we get lost in trying to impress them. Take a breath, be yourself, trust that you are enough. And sing.

Feeling Your Way Through

One of the more common ways to work with the tension that comes with performance anxiety is to place our awareness on the body, repeatedly. Use the breath and the sensations in the body to tune in to the physical being, rather than becoming swept away by the self-conscious mutterings of the mind. Breathe, paying attention to what's happening in the body as we sing, noticing the vibrations in the chest and head; remember to open the chest, allowing more resonance for the sound and more space for the heart to come through in the singing; become aware of the position of your feet, remembering how

rooted we are and that the power of the voice comes from the support we provide when we are in the present. Focus on the naturally arising joy that comes from singing, each phrase shifting the body's vibrations, with innumerable ways to express each and every note.

Sometimes I focus specifically on my feet in the middle of a song. Not only are they full of energy and driving with the rhythm, but they also keep me grounded and centred on the stage.

For these reasons, and because I need to feel the full force of the music coursing through my entire body, I always elect to stand when I am performing. I see many singer-songwriters who, like I do, perform their songs with their voices and their guitars, but many of them choose to sit during their performances. This is fine, of course, and to each his or her own. But I find that playing and singing, especially in the presence of others, can be invigorating to the point of rapture. And rapture isn't something I'm willing to experience sitting down!

Mindful Tune-up

Before taking the stage, let us borrow a line from vulnerability and shame researcher, Brené Brown: 'Don't shrink, don't puff up. Stand in your sacred ground.' Breathe, trust your body. Release your voice and let it sing.

THE FACES IN THE CROWD

Any seasoned performer has experienced the devastating lows of a terrible show and the ethereal highs of those magical evenings when everything clicks. Some of the factors inherent in either experience are beyond our control, but many live inside our heads.

THE MAKE-UP OF THE AUDIENCE MATTERS. If I am singing a song out loud in front of my spouse and children, that involves one level of intimacy. If I am singing a song before a room full of strangers, that's a different type. There's a funny dynamic that happens for some of us where we become the most nervous to sing before those who know us best, often close friends and family. While this isn't always true, it strikes me as curious that we become most anxious before those who know us already, who love us for who we are and are most likely to be supportive of our efforts to sing. Sometimes it seems easier to sing in a room full of one hundred strangers than before ten people I know well.

Standing Room Only, in My Mind

When I was first performing on stage, I used to crack jokes into the microphone about the multitude of empty seats when it was a scarcely attended show, as many of them were. Having eight to ten people in a coffee shop doesn't necessarily feel deserted, but imagine playing to eight or ten people in a venue that's set up to

> ### Mindful Tune-up
>
> Next time you're singing, close your eyes and imagine singing to the sold-out show. Open your heart and feel the expansiveness that comes with sharing your voice on that scale. Then think of a time when someone sang to you. Conjure up a specific memory if you're able, and enjoy those warm feelings that come with being nurtured, being loved. Singing is just another way to love.

seat one hundred. *Awk*-ward. To ease my own sense of discomfort about the situation, I often make use of my sense of humour. And sometimes that can work. Sometimes.

Other times, these attempts at creating laughter come across as patronizing, condescending and ungrateful. Who wants to see a performance (especially if I've paid for the ticket) where the entertainer keeps drawing my attention to the empty seats, implying that my presence is great and all, but certainly not enough to be inspiring.

Along the way I was given some sage advice from a seasoned performer, as he said: It's always a packed house. That's the visual you keep in your mind when you're up on the stage, regardless of how many actual bodies are in attendance. The concert hall is full, you're feeling grateful for each and every one of them in attendance and you're going to sing your heart out for them. Standing room only, in my mind.

Handpick Your Audience

Another trick I have added along the way is that I imagine that not only is each show standing room only, but also in attendance are those I long to impress and those I love most: presidents of record labels, booking agents and perhaps even my favourite songwriters themselves (why, thank you for coming to my show, Paul Simon), and also my closest friends, family and others who tend to bring out the best in me.

I have used this technique each time I can feel my energy wane because of the attendance. Even if the end result was that I gave a good performance to the bar-tender and kitchen staff, at least I can rest comfortably knowing that nothing was wasted. Each of these experiences, from the packed auditorium to the near-empty coffee shop, gives us an opportunity to practise both sides of our mindful singing – the mindfulness and the singing.

We mindful singers have tricks of our own

It's not that easy to keep track of your mind when you're singing in front of other people; distractions are numerous. Our inner critics are likely to be close at hand, ready to silence our voices by making us feel self-conscious. But we mindful singers have tricks of our own and we know how to watch out for the destructive thoughts that creep into our minds; we gently push them aside, returning to our breathing and the song. We do this repeatedly, returning to an awareness of our bodies and our voices again and again.

As we're working with our minds on the stage, let us remember that there is a particular sense of freedom that comes with having a lightly attended performance. It's easier to get away from trying to impress everyone and it can instead be seen as a perfect opportunity to try out newer (or sometimes older) and less polished material. Explore your B- and C-list songs, stretching your voice into places that may be much less familiar. Or try singing familiar songs in new ways, new tempos and new keys. As we know from experience, pushing ourselves past the edge of our comfort zone is where the magic lives.

The Silent Applause

Early in my career, I found myself facing a rather common conundrum: the only venues that would book an 'emerging artist' (code for: has no established fan base) are those that already have a built-in audience, regardless of who is on the stage that evening. These are usually pubs, where people are there for good drink, good friends, good conversation and possibly good music, in that order. That's the kind of show where as a performer, it's not uncommon to go without a single round of applause at the end of a song. No one claps. They just go on laughing, drinking and enjoying themselves.

At first, I was hurt by this. Why aren't they listening? I put my heart and soul into these songs, and I'm sharing them! And these songs I'm singing are really *personal,* dammit! They

mean something (to me!) and you don't even care! (Cue the dramatic music here, diva breaks into sobs.) You can guess what effect these thoughts would have on the singer, how they might affect the voice, the sense of openness or engagement. We've all heard of performers who feel insulted or under-appreciated during their performances, and they end the show abruptly, skulking off the stage in a huff.

Pearls Before Swine

I have an idea. How about instead of just thinking that the audience is there to pay attention to us, we simply focus on the fact that we have a job to do, regardless of the response we receive. Our job is to perform, to sing our hearts out, to give them our best, whether or not they seem to notice.

And the truth is, they may not care about our songs, whether they're personal or not. They may not have heard a single lyric or been moved by that poetic turn of phrase in the third verse that we agonized over for weeks. Like pearls before swine, as they say!

Imagine for a second if we let this victimhood consume us, overtaking that benevolent part of us that wants to share our passion, but also wants to feel appreciated. How would that affect our singing and the energy we put into what we share?

Pushing ourselves past the edge of our comfort zone is where the magic lives

Because the truth is that it's our job to perform. It's not their job to listen. They are under no obligation to pay attention, applaud or even care. They're just there to have fun. It's our job to entertain them. So we catch those thoughts that lead us away from ourselves and our voices, we take a breath, we come back to ourselves. Be here now. And we sing.

Subliminal Effect

Allowing myself to wallow in disappointment is a self-centred way of thinking, and another instance where my brain tells me something other than the truth. Because the larger truth is that the music I was playing, the songs I was sharing, they did matter. They mattered to me, and they had an impact on the audience, even if they didn't acknowledge it with applause. I was providing an atmosphere for the venue. And if I stand here licking my wounds and wondering why they didn't clap, they're going to notice something is amiss.

Whether they acknowledged it or not, they were undoubt-edly being affected by the vibrations I created. In fact it was affecting them on many levels including their mood, the rhythm of their conversation, potentially even the movement of their bodies and the nature of their thoughts, memories and emotions. But that doesn't mean any of it was conscious for them. Or me. And unless I play a song that strikes a special chord with them, chances are they will carry on their merry interactions with very little outward attention to the music.

Interestingly, those same patrons who don't seem to care about my music are often the same ones who, when I cross paths with them later in the evening, are quite appreciative about the music and the mood it provided. The bottom line: contain your thoughts about the listeners. Stay with yourself, your body, your heart, your voice, your mind, your song. When we do that well, we are more likely to draw others towards us. Like gravity, we are all drawn towards open-hearted, compassionate loving-kindness. And when those authentic qualities are coming to us in the form of a song, we can't help but resonate.

◆

We are all affecting the world every moment,

whether we mean to or not. Our actions and states

of mind matter, because we are so deeply

interconnected with one another.

FROM 'BEING LOVE'
RAM DASS

◆

CHAPTER FIVE

MOVING BEYOND

*In the middle of the song, when I'm in the flow,
I'm aware of the rhythm more than anything. It is
within me, without me, surrounding me, it is me. I'm
aware of other people too, but mostly I'm aware of the
music, and the unstoppable, pulsating rhythm. In the
finest moments of a live performance, the song is
playing me, not the other way around. I'm not making
the music, I'm just letting it come through. The music
may be collared by the vessel through which
it passes, but it is most certainly coming
not from, but through.*

THE DOORS ARE OPEN

◆

As we know by now, music and singing have tremendous power to transform our thoughts, our emotions, and as we'll explore shortly, our consciousness. This art we are creating is serious business, and there is a multitude of avenues worthy of further exploration.

A s we enter into this final chapter, it's appropriate to both wrap things up and to do just the opposite, throwing open the doors. Our journey with mindful singing is just beginning, and it's up to us to decide where we go from here, given the numerous possible directions. Different exercises, new ways of connecting with our voices, using our voices to connect with others, exploring avenues for keeping our musical interest piqued, the options before us seem limitless. And in many ways they are, leaving us only limited by the reaches of our own creativity.

Now that we're reconnecting with our voices in this mindful approach to singing, we can use the same basic tools to follow our voices wherever they lead. Just as the mindfulness

◆

Music can change the world
because music can change people.

Bono
IRISH SINGER-SONGWRITER AND MUSICIAN

◆

that comes with daily meditation is designed to be carried with us throughout our day, the same is true for the regular practice of mindful singing. By remembering to slow down, to breathe, to stand tall with an open heart and to relish the deep vibrational joy we create in our bodies when we sing, we can't help but carry this wherever we go. Keep singing, keep buzzing, keep humming and whistling and listening to music. You're in charge of the soundtrack. Get on it.

By this point in our journey, you're very much aware of the ability of mindful singing to awaken our bodies, minds, hearts and spirits, bringing us into the present and enriching our lives. One additional realm to explore involves an altered state of consciousness, one where time feels suspended and the experience of oneness is sublime.

Flow

My brother and I were both very athletic when in our youth, changing sports with the seasons, always involved in something. Most of my childhood idols wore professional sports kit, though some of them wore country club attire as they made their way around the golf course. Names like Michael Jordan, Pelé and Ken Griffey Jr. were spoken with reverence in my home, their professional accomplishments legendary.

As I grew older, I noticed a common dimension among these achievers when they were performing at their best: they were undeniably focused, but seemingly relaxed at the same time. 'I felt like I couldn't miss,' said the basketball player who just poured in fifty points. 'Time disappeared,' said the track star. 'I just ran.' This same type of relaxed focus seemed also to overtake my mother at certain times, losing herself in her sewing room, producing a mind-boggling array of well-stitched items in no time at all. While I recognized this interesting phenomenon, it wasn't until my adulthood that I started understanding what was going on. That's true in many different ways.

Finding Flow Through Music

As we have explored, the simple act of using our voices has a profound impact on our lives and the lives of those around us. Singing brings us into the present, increasing our awareness of our bodies, our voices, our minds and our realities. And while singing certainly increases feelings of well-being and happiness, it also has the power to take us beyond these feelings into a blissful dimension that a renowned Hungarian psychologist calls the state of 'optimal experience', also known as 'flow'.

Best-selling author Mihaly Csikszentmihalyi builds his research upon the heart of mindfulness: 'a person can make himself happy, or miserable, regardless of what is actually happening "outside", just by changing the contents of consciousness'. One of the best ways of changing consciousness, he posits, is to put ourselves into a state of flow.

'Flow' is characterized by a state of intense focus and deep concentration, where nothing else matters because the mind is fully immersed in the present activity. In these spaces, self-consciousness disappears, time can become distorted and we become all-absorbed in the present activity. It involves an active type of engagement that strikes the perfect balance between challenge and skill. If a task is too challenging for our present skill set, we become anxious and worried and we're tempted to give up. If it's too easy, we grow bored. But as these two elements converge in a way that is fully engaging, we may find ourselves in a blissful state of flow.

Like a rock climber with laser-like focus on a challenging climbing route; a basketball player whose aim is 'locked in' and feels like she can't miss; the singer on the stage who has transcended space and time, enrapturing each of his listeners, who are hanging on his every note. Being in a state of flow makes us feel ecstatic, even if we appear calm to others on the outside. Singing is a perfect vehicle to bring us home, tune us in and engage us in this optimal state.

Creating Flow

How do we, as mindful singers, make it happen? Well, if I knew the precise answer, I might be writing a different type of book. The truth is that although I have performed hundreds of times, I have felt that 'music is playing me' sensation only a handful of times. But I do know the feeling of losing myself for hours while playing the guitar, writing or recording a song. Nothing else matters when we're happily absorbed in something we love.

Putting ourselves into a position to get into the flow involves practice, dedication and mindfulness. We need to put in the practice time so that muscle memory can take over when we're performing, allowing us to relax on stage. The dedication is both to ourselves and our craft. We can't go into a live performance with the goal of getting into the flow. It's something that has the possibility of happening when all the right factors are present. One of these is the audience and their connection with you and with the music. Another is our sense of presence and how we work with our nerves on the stage. Any activity that involves human beings is inherently unpredictable. But if you're interested in experiencing the flow through singing, go for it. Sing daily, start performing in front of others and with others, then keep doing it as long as it brings you joy. Do it long enough and eventually you'll have one of those magical nights that neither you nor the audience will forget, when time was suspended and the only things in existence were the music, rhythm and love.

OTHER AVENUES

The ideas and exercises contained within these pages are just the beginning for you. This introduction to mindful singing will now allow you to spread your vocal wings as far as you like, following your musical heart in any number of creative directions.

I WAS INITIALLY RELUCTANT a few years ago when a mentor of mine approached me with an opportunity to teach Gestalt Therapy to graduate students. I hadn't formally taught before, and although I had earned a certificate in the subject, I questioned the depth of my teachable knowledge. He reminded me that what I had to offer the students was Gestalt, Jeremy-style. And that I could do. Which is just like mindful singing at this stage of the game. It's time to make it yours, put your stamp on it and to give yourself the permission to explore wherever your musical spirit leads you.

As you scroll through the following list of ways to create your own path to mindful singing, I encourage you to pay attention to both types of charged reactions – notice those things you are inherently drawn to, as well as those that instantly frighten or repel you. Both likely hold something worthy of a second look.

The following is a small sample of ways to take mindful singing further:

• Take vocal lessons. It's humbling to put our voices out there, but if we can move our egos aside, learning from a trained professional can make for stronger and more finely controlled singing voices.

• Write a song. Or several. There are many ways to begin, and many free online resources. Search 'How to write a song'. It's not as hard as you think.

• Do daily exercises to strengthen your control over your singing muscles.

• Learn an instrument, so you can accompany yourself.

• Use online resources: the internet is full of free videos and instructions for singing, as well as learning any instrument.

Mindful Tune-up

Take a full inhalation and, while holding your breath, move your abdominal muscles in and out four times, then release the breath. Do the same thing while holding the out breath, before taking another inhalation. This strengthens the diaphragm and the other singing muscles.

- Read poetry, exposing yourself to the beauty and magic of the written word, feeling the rhythm of the phrase, the sound of the vowels; these are good things for our musical soul.

- Expose yourself to new music. Search the internet, ask your friends, even your kids. More people are making and recording music than ever before and you have access to most of it. Regardless of the type of music that you love, the odds are good that there are plenty of contemporary musicians you have never heard of who are making the kind of music you would absolutely enjoy.

- Go and listen to live music. Even if seeing live music isn't your thing or they don't play the kind of music you like where you live, I still urge you to go. Attend a performance, enjoy the street musicians, just expose yourself to a live human being making music in the moment. Let yourself be moved by that. Connecting through music is healing.

- Listen to a cappella music. Listen to the amazing sounds the singers get from their voices. If you can hear them, learn to sing harmony lines in addition to the main melody.

- Train your ear. There are a variety of online apps and resources available to help. The better our ear, the more likely we are to sing on pitch.

- Explore the wonders of Tibetan singing bowls as a sonic combination of mindfulness, breath and sound.

- Men: develop your falsetto voice. Some falsely think of singing in that high range as being too feminine for men, but it's beautiful and requires a great deal of breath support. Set aside your judgement, relax your throat and try singing in the uppermost end of your vocal range.

• Meditate – you won't regret it. To paraphrase author Dr Wayne Dyer, sit quietly for ten minutes once every day. And if you're too busy for that, do it twice a day.

• Start hosting your own music night in your home, even if it's just two or three friends who sing or play an instrument. Share songs, sing songs or take turns sharing recordings of your favourite songs. We all connect to music differently, and a single song can make for interesting discussion afterwards about the memories, feelings and associations that come up when we listen. Make music night a regular thing. Rotate houses. Invite others along who love music, make music or are simply curious. You'll be surprised at what happens.

• Bring your new mindful principles with you as you expand your singing circle.

Power in Numbers

Despite all our flaws, we can all agree that human beings are capable of some pretty spectacular things. And this is never more true than when we combine our gifts and harness the power of the group. As much as I can be moved by the simple beauty of a solo performer, the addition of even one more voice adds far more than simply doubling the sound. The interplay between voices, the magic of the duo, is more than the sum of its parts.

There are several ways in which we, as mindful singers, can bring a sense of presence into the group experience, and as you've already guessed, it begins with our own ability to embody this mindfulness ourselves, moment-by-moment. Or as much as we're able to do so. We breathe, we feel into the presence of our bodies as we're singing or playing, we open our hearts, relax our voices, support the breath … you remember how it's done. First and foremost, we strive to remember this again and again, because it becomes easy to forget when we are around other people, especially while making music. It's easy to lose ourselves and to forget to breathe. So start there. Breathe often, with awareness. Feel your body. Move. Relax. Breathe again. Sing. Smile. This is fun.

As we get connected with some of the other singers, we could introduce some easy mindful ideas to the group. Share your own experience, invite everyone to do the square breath a few times. Keep it simple. Encourage them to tune in to their bodies and breathe while they're playing or singing.

I have known bands who collectively discovered the power of meditation and benefited from the impact it had on their music. They began every rehearsal, performance or recording session with a group meditation. Nothing fancy, just a few minutes of silence, noticing the breath, watching the mind, observing the thoughts and returning to the breath. Again. And again. Be Here Now. I saw one such band play a show and they were very much alive, embodied – and absolutely joyful.

You Got This

Beginnings and endings are one and the same, constant companions, never one without the other. We can't say goodbye to something without saying hello to something else, even if we don't know what that something else is quite yet. Let the ritual of turning the last page of this final chapter serve as a beginning for the next chapter of your own mindful journey. Your voice is sacred, singing is important and where you take things from here is up to you. However you choose to use your voice from this point forward, whether a regular singer or not, may mindfulness continue to be a part of it.

As we come to the conclusion of our journey together (for now), let me say that it has been a supreme honour for me to be here with you. I was eager to write this book, I was happy to have it published and I am most grateful that you've read it. If you enjoyed it, please tell your friends. Or buy them a copy. Or three. Especially three. Soon we'll all be singing and living more mindfully and that could make a palpable difference.

Singing has been transformative in my life and I know some of you will find this to be true as well as long as you keep at it. Our voices are magical, much more so than we tend to think. So please, for all of us, don't let the music stop. Keep singing. The rest of us are counting on it. Thank you in advance.

BIBLIOGRAPHY

BIBLIOGRAPHY

Csikszentmihalyi, Mihaly. *Flow: The Psychology of Optimal Experience* (HarperCollins, New York, 1990)

Dass, Ram. *Being Love* (www.ramdass.org/being-love)

Jenny, Hans. *Cymatics: A Study of Wave Phenomena and Vibration*, 3rd Edition (Macromedia Press, San Francisco, 2001)

Jesperson, Otto. *Language: Its Nature, Development and Origin* (G. Allen & Unwin Ltd, London, 1922)

Leeds, Joshua. *The Power of Sound* (Healing Arts Press, Rochester, Vermont, 2001)

Miller, James R. *Visions From Earth* (Trafford Publishing, Bloomington, Indiana, 2004)

Rilke, Rainer Maria. *Rilke's Book of Hours: Love Poems to God*, translated by Joanna Macy and Anita Barrows, (Riverhead Books, New York, 2004)

Sondheim, Stephen. *Sweeney Todd: The Demon Barber of Fleet Street* (1979)

Stojanovic, Dejan. *The Sun Watches the Sun* (New Avenue Books, 2012)

Thích Nhat Hanh. *Peace Is Every Step* (Random House Publishing, New York, 1992)

INDEX

ACKNOWLEDGEMENTS

◆

To author Clea Dannan for getting all of this started; to the
savvy editors and designers at Leaping Hare Press for working their magic;
to my parents for singing to me; to my grandmother for teaching me how to dance;
to the innumerable friends, family members, colleagues, musicians, authors,
songwriters, clients and tormentors along the way who helped me find
my own voice; and of course to Avery, my constant source of light
and inspiration: my deepest gratitude, I love you all.